The Asset Economy

The Asset Economy

Property Ownership and the New Logic of Inequality

Lisa Adkins, Melinda Cooper
and Martijn Konings

polity

First published in 2020 by Polity Press

Polity Press
65 Bridge Street
Cambridge CB2 1UR, UK

Polity Press
101 Station Landing
Suite 300
Medford, MA 02155, USA

ISBN-13: 978-1-5095-4345-8
ISBN-13: 978-1-5095-4346-5 (pb)

A catalogue record for this book is available from the British Library.

Library of Congress Cataloging-in-Publication Data
Names: Adkins, Lisa, 1966- author. | Konings, Martijn, 1975- author. | Cooper, Melinda, author.
Title: The asset economy : property ownership and the new logic of inequality / Lisa Adkins, Martijn Konings and Melinda Cooper.
Description: Medford : Polity Press, 2020. | Includes bibliographical references and index. | Summary: "How assets dictate the new class system"-- Provided by publisher. Identifiers: LCCN 2020013339 (print) | LCCN 2020013340 (ebook) | ISBN 9781509543458 (hardback) | ISBN 9781509543465 (paperback) | ISBN 9781509543472 (epub) | ISBN 9781509544226 (adobe pdf)
Subjects: LCSH: Home ownership--Social aspects. | Generation Y--Social conditions. | Social stratification. | Finance--Social aspects. | Time--Social aspects.
Classification: LCC HD7287.8 .A35 2020 (print) | LCC HD7287.8 (ebook) | DDC 306.3--dc23
LC record available at https://lccn.loc.gov/2020013339
LC ebook record available at https://lccn.loc.gov/2020013340

Typeset in 11 on 13 pt Sabon
by Fakenham Prepress Solutions, Fakenham, Norfolk NR21 8NL
Printed and bound in Great Britain by CPI Group (UK) Ltd, Croydon

For further information on Polity, visit our website:
politybooks.com

Contents

Preface

The collaboration that led to the writing of this book emerged out of the convergence of ideas from our individual work. Each of our recent books (Adkins' *The Time of Money*, Cooper's *Family Values* and Konings' *Capital and Time*) emphasized the growing role that speculative, asset-centred economic logics play in contemporary society. In this book we aim to build on that work to develop a new way of thinking about class and inequality.

We are very grateful for the generous institutional support that this project has received from the Faculty of Arts and Social Sciences at the University of Sydney, in particular its FutureFix programme 'Asset Ownership and the New Inequality'.

In what follows, we make frequent reference to the 2007–8 financial crisis. Since that event, the inequalities associated with asset-based wealth have become more entrenched. As this book goes to press, the world is experiencing a very different kind of emergency – the Covid-19 pandemic. In numerous countries, death rates are soaring, governments have put in place stay-at-home and social distancing mandates, and millions have lost their jobs as businesses are shutting down. The crisis has also done much to draw attention to existing levels of inequality. While the wealthy are able to take refuge in holiday homes, many workers living paycheck to paycheck cannot afford to 'socially isolate'. Somewhere in between is a middle class that, mostly able to ride out the storm by staying inside, may be counting its blessings but is at the same time increasingly aware of how precarious its security – financial and otherwise – really is.

Central banks have stepped up their asset purchase programmes, pushing the scale and scope of 'quantitative easing' to new levels. The \$2 trillion relief package which Trump approved at the end of March 2020, even as he was still playing down the public health aspect of the pandemic, works largely according to the logic of trickle-down economics, offering financial help to embattled firms in the hope that this will induce them to maintain employment. Other countries, including the UK and Canada, have guaranteed wages directly. Such moves have fuelled hopes for a more enduring revival of Keynesianism or even for a radical programme of progressive economic policy. But even though crises can widen the horizon of political possibility, we should not forget how in the aftermath of the 2007–8 crisis, the hoped-for return to Keynesianism was quickly transformed into virulent austerity politics.

The political stakes will be even higher this time. If the post-Covid-19 era sees another wave of asset inflation, and if home ownership remains the only real – but less and less realistic – way for ordinary people to participate in that logic, the next decade will see a continuation of the social and political polarization that has been such a defining feature of the past decade.

Introduction

At the start of 2019, *The Economist* coined the term 'millennial socialism' to refer to the growth of strong, critical and left-wing sentiments in a generation that until recently was primarily known for its sense of entitlement and its obsession with social media. It noted that a large percentage of young people hold a favourable view of socialism and that '[i]n the primaries in 2016 more young folk voted for Bernie Sanders than for Hillary Clinton and Donald Trump combined'. *The Economist* acknowledged that some of these millennials may have good reasons for their political sentiments. But it immediately went on to declare that understanding this trend shouldn't lead us to justify or legitimate it – socialism remains as dangerous as, according to the magazine, it always has been. It views millennial socialism as being too 'pessimistic' and as wanting things that are 'politically dangerous'. While voicing some qualified appreciation for millennial socialism's 'refreshing willingness to challenge the status quo', *The Economist* strongly denounced its naïve 'faith in the incorruptibility of collective action'. The *Sydney Morning Herald* followed up in the same month with an opinion piece arguing that while millennial socialism has roots in millennials' 'rising anxiety about their economic prospects' (and in particular the virtual impossibility of ever attaining home ownership in the country's largest cities), as a political choice it seemed to reflect above all ignorance and the lack of memory of the horrors of Communism (Switzer 2019).

The attention that the millennial generation's political positioning has received from establishment media outlets is testimony to an emergent reality. But the framing of this political shift in terms of a generational schism would seem to rest on flimsy conceptual foundations. Indeed, while generational analysis may be making a return to public debate, among social scientists it has largely gone out of fashion. The idea that being born around the same time or experiencing the same historical events at the same age produces a natural solidarity or a similar experience of life is now considered overly simplistic. It is typically seen as too abstracted from a range of other structural inequalities that would seem to have far greater bearing on people's position in the social hierarchy. Just as there are poor baby boomers, so there are fabulously wealthy millennials.

Yet some element of generational distinction seems to be playing an undeniable role in the logic of the present. So, what do we make of this? A useful direction here was indicated in the *Financial Times* (2019), which is always more willing to put critical analysis to work for the preservation of capitalism. Featuring a picture of economist and former chair of the US Federal Reserve Ben Bernanke juxtaposed with one of millennial Democratic politician Alexandria Ocasio-Cortez, one of its opinion pieces stated that 'Quantitative Easing was the Father of Millennial Socialism'. Quantitative easing is a policy that central banks in many countries have relied on over the past decade to rekindle economic growth and escape from the Great Recession that ensued in the wake of the financial crisis of 2007–8. It works on the idea that, if central banks push large amounts of liquidity into the financial system, banks and other financial institutions will lend more liberally and so spur investment, growth and employment. But one of the main points of critique of these policies has been that this transmission mechanism is not in fact working very well, and that in practice quantitative easing has propped up the values of financial assets *without* translating into higher rates of employment and growth (Blyth 2013; Gane 2015). That is to say, quantitative easing is often seen as working to enrich the owners of financial assets (often pejoratively referred to as 'rentiers') at the expense of those who have to work for a living.

The same *Financial Times* piece continued with an observation on the generational effects of property prices. Noting the dramatic divergence between wages and property prices in large cities over the past decade (not just in New York and San Francisco but also in many smaller urban centres), it concluded: 'The young are locked out.' In almost all large Western urban centres, property prices have reached levels that make renting very expensive and put home ownership effectively out of reach for many. Although housing is by no means the only asset that plays an important role in the contemporary political economy, it plays a central role in the story that we tell in the following pages. Property inflation in large urban centres is the linchpin of a new logic of inequality.

Property price inflation is not limited to the past decade. In major cities across the Western world property prices have been on the rise for several decades. If this problem had been limited to the past decade, we would just be looking at a particularly inappropriate set of policies conceived by incompetent or corrupt elites. That would be bad enough, but we might reasonably hope that greater awareness of the issue would lead to democratic pushback and a reversal of quantitative easing policies. But the problem is of longer standing and reaches deeper into the fabric of social life. As we will see in the following pages, quantitative easing is only a more explicit version of financial policies that have been pursued since the 1980s that aim to make asset ownership profitable. We should also not be too quick to cast this as a project that aimed to enrich a tiny elite at the expense of the rest of the population, as the current focus on the runaway wealth of the 1% would suggest. The phenomenon of the 1% pulling away from the rest of society is all too real, but it is so thorny and intractable precisely because it is anchored in a wider institutional and social configuration that has generated particular constituencies with a vested interest in these sorts of policies.

It is therefore important here not to reach too quickly for a critique of 'rentierism'. It may be a useful means of expressing moral opprobrium and voicing concern about a world that allows some to receive income without having to work for it, but its analytical edge is blunt. The critique of rentierism is long-standing. It has for many years been a favourite tool of the left, whether of middle-of-the-road progressive reformists, labour politics, or more radical currents. Indeed, it had been one of John Maynard Keynes' stated concerns to ensure the 'euthanasia of the rentier' (Keynes 1936: 376), and it seemed to many that mid-twentieth-century capitalism had delivered precisely this, bringing capitalism in line with the needs of working people. But the past decades have done much to erode this sense that capital can work to advance the interests of society as a whole. Left-wing critics have relied on the critique of unproductive rentierism to criticize neoliberalism since its inception (Duménil & Lévy 2005; Onaran et al. 2011; Standing 2016), but in recent years the critique of rentierism has returned to mainstream public debate with Thomas Piketty's (2014) book *Capital in the Twenty-First Century*.

Piketty sees the growth of inequality primarily in terms of the rentier fortunes of those at the very top. In this book we argue that this is only part of a larger story that we need to understand. By framing present-day trends in terms of a return to the days before the Keynesian euthanasia of the rentier, we argue that Piketty ultimately understates the qualitatively different logic governing the mechanisms of inequality production in current times. It is certainly important to understand how the escalation of inequality at the very top has been able to continue for so long in a democratic society, but we need to recognize it as part of a wider, more structural reconfiguration of patterns of inequality. After all, the advent of mass democracy was one of the key pressures that led to the levelling policies of the New Deal and post-war state. To a significant extent, the 'rentier function' has become embedded across social life as a whole. But the growing awareness that owning assets often pays more than working for a living has not yet been translated into a new understanding of class and inequality. Although the phenomenon of property inflation has received plenty of commentary, when it comes to thinking about class, inequality and stratification in more systematic ways we often tend to revert to older models based on work and occupation.

The key element shaping inequality is no longer the employment relationship, but rather whether one is able to buy assets that appreciate at a faster rate than both inflation and wages. Employment remains an important factor as it shapes the ability to purchase assets (e.g.

the ability to service a mortgage), but it is increasingly only one among other factors. Of course, income from work remains vitally important for many people as a way to access subsistence goods, but the important point is that by itself it is less and less able to serve as the basis of what most people would consider a middle-class lifestyle. Asset appreciation has been engendered by a specific institutional nexus that has fundamentally redrawn the social structure – such that asset ownership is now becoming more important than employment as a determinant of class position.

The millennial generation is the first to experience this reality in its full force. So, the generational aspect is important not because it produces a uniform experience of social life or a clean divide between different genera-tions (as a naïve approach to generational analysis would imply), but precisely because it is where the economic fault-lines that four decades of neoliberal fiscal and financial policies have produced are becoming visible. After all, some millennials have access to parental wealth (often itself the result of property inflation) that allows them to buy into dynamics of asset inflation. What we are seeing in the present era is the growing importance of intergenerational transfer and inher-itance for the determination of life chances.

Crucially, however, this is not best understood as a return to an earlier era, when property was passed on (generally among men) from one generation to another in a more or less stable and mostly uneventful way. Inheritance is no longer a simple transmission of property titles, but increasingly a strategically timed transfer of funds that need to be leveraged and put to work in the speculative logic of the asset economy. This new logic of inequality has mixed 'hypercapi-talist' logics of financialization with 'feudal' logics of inheritance to reshape the social class structure as a whole. The generational dimension interacts with the speculative logic of the contemporary financial system to shape asset-based lifetimes.

Plan of the book

In the following chapters, we will show how the changing role of assets has been responsible for the creation of a new logic of inequality in Anglo-capitalist societies. In the next chapter, 'Asset Logics', we explain the importance of thinking of the contemporary economic system as dominated by the logic of assets. We differentiate our approach from competing perspectives that tend to overemphasize the orthodox image of the market and in particular the idea that liquidity is an inherent aspect of financialization. Such perspectives neglect the fact that participation in the financialized economy often involves (and regularly necessitates) making highly illiquid investments. The typical economic actor needs to take on debt in order to finance an asset purchase and then needs to pay down the debt over an extended period of time, relying on returns and capital gains from the asset as well as separate earnings from work. As the latter stagnate, the role of speculative asset gains becomes more and more important (both to the quality of individual and household balance sheets and to overall macroeconomic performance and policy).

The chapter then turns to Piketty's observation that the growth of asset values has outstripped returns on labour over the past four decades. This is a key point of reference for our book, but Piketty's account has two key weaknesses. First, he understands the tendency for capital income to exceed labour income as the reassertion of a basic law of capital rather than as an outcome of a series of transformations in fiscal and monetary policy that have shifted inflationary pressures from consumer prices and wages to asset prices. The chapter indicates some of the key aspects of this policy configuration, which are examined in more detail in the following chapter, 'The Making of the Asset Economy'. Second, Piketty's focus and that of others following his analysis has been skewed towards the very top layers of the population (the 1%), and they have generally not pursued the implications for a more general understanding of class and stratification. This is where some distance is needed from the idea that the current era represents a return to classic liberalism or a 'new gilded age'. Contemporary inequality in Western countries is built on a base of middle-class asset ownership that evolved during the post-New Deal and post-war era. This is especially evident in the area of housing: the sustained inflation of property values over several decades has fundamentally shifted the social class structure, from a logic that was structured around employment towards one that is organized around participation in asset ownership and appreciation.

The next chapter, 'The Making of the Asset Economy', discusses the origins and development of asset inflation in more detail, aiming to understand how we arrived in a situation where continuous asset price inflation has replaced wage inflation as a key economic driver. To this end, it returns to the 1970s, a decade that saw historic declines in asset prices as consumer price inflation cut into the returns on assets, combined with the growth of wages and welfare state expenditure as trade unions sought to keep up with or even outpace the rise in consumer prices. Over the next decades, this combination of high wage inflation and asset price depreciation was reversed. The chapter examines the role of monetary policy, taxation policy (notably capital gains taxation) and public spending constraints as the primary levers by which this reversal was effected and the asset inflation/wage stagnation norm was forged. This chapter also elucidates the role of Third Way neoliberals such as Bill Clinton in the US, Tony Blair in the UK and Paul Keating in Australia in softening, but also consolidating, this new policy regime by offering consumer credit as a pathway towards democratized capital gains – a kind of asset-owning democracy. Anticipated by Margaret Thatcher and Ronald Reagan, Third Way neoliberals offered up the hope that we could all participate in asset price appreciation, via a democratization of stock ownership, home ownership, or simply ownership of our own skills (our 'human capital'). The Third Way take on human capital theory imagined that, by adopting an entrepreneurial investor stance towards life, people could compensate for stagnant income from labour through income from their human capital on a permanent basis and that this could altogether neutralize the antagonism between employees and employers. Fiscal and monetary policy became heavily driven by the notion that life course events such as education, housing and employment are above all to be seen as investment opportunities.

The final chapter in this book, 'New Class Realities', shows how forty years of asset inflation and wage stagnation have exposed the limits of this Third Way vision. It is in housing, already widely distributed across the population (at least in Anglo-American countries) at the start of the neoliberal era, where the promise of inclusion in capital gains has mostly played out. The combination of rising house prices, low interest rates and the democratization of mortgage credit has meant that substantial parts of populations in Anglo-capitalist countries have been able to participate in asset-based capital gains. But the reality of this has been both less utopian and less universal than that projected by the architects of the democratized asset ownership project. Home ownership has just as often entailed greater reliance on stagnant wages as it has meant economic independence. Only the top layer of the population, holding diversified asset portfolios that benefit from various forms of preferential tax treatment, may be said to approximate an ideal of asset ownership. Moreover, the very logic of asset appreciation means that growing segments are unable to buy into it.

Increasingly, the only way to buy property in major Western cities is with parental assistance. The division between people who do and do not have access to parental wealth is becoming particularly evident as a fault-line in the 'millennial' generation, who are the first since the post-war boom to really experience the impossibility of building up wealth and securing access to a middle-class lifestyle on the basis of wage-labour alone. The chapter pushes back against the trend to couch this in purely generational terms. After all, a millennial who is likely to inherit real estate or to receive a cash transfer from parents for a deposit on a property is far more advantaged than either a renting boomer or a millennial without access to parental wealth. In other words, intergenerational transfers have become a key mechanism in the new logic of *class*. The chapter develops an analysis of the patterns of stratification and exclusion generated by the asset economy, including their cultural and affective impacts. It conceptualizes class not (as it has been traditionally) in terms of people's relationship to work and education, but rather in terms of their relationship to assets. Contemporary life is increasingly ordered by the speculative dynamics of the asset economy and in particular by the double dynamic of appreciation and depreciation.

In the Conclusion, we reflect on the wider implications of the rise of the asset economy. Key here is the way in which economic policies are interacting with imperatives of political legitimation. Policies (capital gains tax discounts, low interest rates) that cater to a core constituency of asset-owning citizens increasingly have the effect of preventing new entry to this constituency. However, policies that aim to make property more affordable not only tend to be electorally troublesome, but also result in lower rates of economic growth in general and jeopardize the growth of employment. Consequently, few governments can resist policies that reflate the housing market, thereby fuelling the growth of asset-led inequality even as it appears these instruments are losing some of their effectiveness and require more firepower with each round. It is against this economic background that key aspects of the political shifts and turmoil of the past decade need to be seen, and we conclude by asking what it may mean for Anglo-capitalist societies and their citizens if the same logic remains operative.

Asset Logics

From commodity logics to asset logics

What does it mean to understand the contemporary economic system as dominated by the logic of assets? It is useful here to contrast our approach with a more common way of characterizing the socio-economic shifts of the neoliberal era – one that emphasizes the logic of commodification and how it has undermined the non-market institutions of the post-New Deal and post-war era. That approach, while typically highly critical of mainstream economics, nonetheless reproduces too many of its framing concepts. By understanding economic mechanisms primarily in terms of commodity exchange, it attributes too much reality to the mainstream image of the market.

This commodification model remains overly indebted to what Minsky (1982: 61) refers to as the 'village fair' model of neoclassical economics, where people meet to exchange goods to mutual benefit. They may use money to facilitate the process, but this does not undermine the fundamentally barter-like character of the system: money is simply a device to cut down on the number of intermediating exchanges required and to arrive at an optimal redistribution more efficiently. It may be understood that this is a recurrent process, but each round is nonetheless conceived as self-contained, with an identifiable starting point and an endpoint that brings the process to a conclusion. In other words, each round of commodity exchange starts out with all the participants arriving with a clean slate, and they leave the same way, leaving no scores to be settled or debts to negotiate for the next round (Shackle 1972). This means that the model does not incorporate relations of credit and debt and is unable to recognize the temporally situated interdependence of economic actors. It sees merely a series of presents, and fails to recognize the existence of a past or future in the way we typically understand those dimensions; that is, a past that isn't merely an external resource constraint but is significant because we made certain investments and a future that is uncertain and requires us to make choices without having all the information we would like to have. In other words, this model, by taking the commodity as the paradigmatic form of the capitalist economy, lacks a temporal dimension that would allow us to understand uncertainty and speculation as constitutive aspects of economic life (Cooper & Konings 2015).

That orthodox economics can build internally consistent models without needing credit and debt, or indeed even money, was famously demonstrated by the Arrow–Debreu model in the 1950s. Since that time, orthodox economics has explored numerous avenues in order to take credit, money and finance more seriously, given their obvious real-world importance, especially over the past half-century. But heterodox perspectives have always insisted that such attempts have never amounted to more than unconvincing attempts to paper over a basic problem. A key plank of the critique of mainstream economics (as well as of neoliberalism as a real-world force) has been the emphasis on the constitutive significance of finance and the way it upends claims about the efficiency of markets.

However, although it is common among heterodox political economists to ridicule the idea that the contemporary capitalist system can be analysed by relying on the model of the barter economy (Keen 2011), by and large they have found it difficult to move beyond the paradigm of the commodity form. Like mainstream economists, they have continued to model the role of finance and debt on the idea of commodification, in the sense that the proliferation of relations of credit and debt is seen as an extension of the logic of the commodity and exchange (Hudson 2012; Lapavitsas 2009, 2014; Strange 1988). Where they differ from mainstream economists is in their insistence that there is something excessive, unsustainable or dysfunctional about this expansion. In Polanyian terms, the contemporary growth of finance reflects the irrational commodification of money, a movement whereby the measure of commodities is being turned into a commodity itself and the market starts to 'disembed' itself from society (Block & Somers 2014; Fraser & Jaeggi 2018; Streeck 2014). The growth of credit and debt is seen as a sign of the unsustainable extent of commodification: as demonstrating that commodification, when its logic becomes universalized, does not lead to an idyllic village fair but has destabilizing consequences.

While such critiques have been valuable in highlighting the ways in which financialized capitalism fails to correspond to the model of an efficient market, they are also limited in ways that have become more apparent as the contours of the asset economy have become more visible. Theoretically, if we understand economic processes through the lens of the commodity, there is simply no inherent need or organic place for finance. And as a consequence, we will find it difficult to move beyond strongly normative assessments that understand finance as dysfunctional, speculative and parasitic. Indeed, by focusing so strongly on the quantitative dimension of the expansion of finance, these critiques are unable to shed much light on the qualitative transformations that financialization has effected.

In many ways, the commodity is an anachronistic lens through which to understand the character of present-day economic restructuring. This has been intimated for some time now by those who have mapped how the commodity form has transformed in our present era: rather than entirely closed off or fixed objects, here commodities are cast as open, in-motion, processual and relational in character (Berardi 2011; Boltanski & Chiapello 2005; Thrift 2008). While we are sympathetic to such attempts to reconceptualize the commodity, we see no need to remain within the restrictive parameters that it imposes. Recent work focusing on the logic of capitalization and securitization brings us much closer to the specific economic modalities of the neoliberal era. Bringing the dimension of time into the heart of the analysis, this body of work argues that capitalization works through the constitution, in the present, of a claim on anticipated future revenue flows that is supported by legal instruments as well as wider institutional conditions. What occurs here is a shift in focus from the commodity as the locus of value towards an understanding of value as speculative (Muniesa 2011). Value is always an expectation-driven practice of valuation oriented towards an uncertain future. These ideas have received useful elaboration in the work of social scientists who locate the drivers of the process of assetization in a series of socio-technical calculative devices, especially those associated with business, accounting and financial valuations (see, for example, Birch 2017; Doganova & Muniesa 2015; Leyshon & Thrift 2007; Muniesa 2016; Muniesa et al. 2017). Such devices transform 'things' into income-generating assets whose value in the present is calculated on the basis of yet-to-be-actualized future income streams.

Although these perspectives go quite a long way towards displacing the dominance of the commodity as a paradigm of political economy, in some ways they have remained beholden to the image of 'the market'. They tend to associate the logic of finance with the growth of liquidity and they often treat market liquidity as if this were an inherent property of expanding financial markets. The liquidity paradigm becomes particularly problematic when it comes to understanding the expansion of finance into everyday life, as it misleadingly models the way in which households participate in the financialized economy on an image of the fluid world of high finance. Crucially, participation in the financialized economy often involves making highly *illiquid* investments. That is why it is more appropriate to refer to an asset economy than a debt economy or a financialized economy. So, while the driving assumption found in many analyses of the financialization of daily life is that this process involves an effective and continuous integration of households into the liquidity of finance (see, for example, Martin 2002), in reality it involves a merging of finance with a logic of household investment that is far clunkier. The asset economy requires not low-commitment participation in trading, but investment and exposure (Feher 2018).

An asset is a property title that must be constantly valued as a balance sheet item but often precisely cannot be readily traded. An asset has a particular temporal structure: it requires an upfront investment of (often borrowed) funds and it is meant to generate returns over a particular future timeframe. The neoliberal household is what we refer to as a Minskyan unit, an economic entity that needs to take speculative positions by borrowing funds and ensure that it is able to meet the repayments due on its debts (Adkins 2019). If liquidity could always be assumed, the financialized economy would work essentially like a commodity economy and households would never have to experience financing problems or constraints. Nor would it be very likely that the benefits of financialization could have been distributed as unequally as in fact they are. After all, in a fully liquid world there would be no reason for anyone to hang on to assets that are subject to devaluation over a longer period of time, just as such a world would not have buy-in thresholds that limit participation in markets to the already well off. The generic capitalization model cannot explain the dynamics of simultaneous asset appreciation and depreciation – or, to put it more precisely, it is unable to explain why some economic actors are more systematically exposed to the devaluation and appreciation of specific assets than other people.

Minskyan households

To refer to the contemporary household as a Minskyan unit is to say that in the asset economy the household exists no longer primarily as a unit of subsistence or consumption but increasingly as a balance sheet of assets and liabilities that must be managed. This is reflected in the specific forms of financial stress that middle-class households nowadays experience, which increasingly relate not just to the possibility of accessing basic subsistence items (although this may well be present too), but derive from the specific pressures involved in managing balance sheet exposures and the problems involved in building up wealth over time. The instability of the financialized economy means that the household balance sheet requires constant rebalancing (Bryan & Rafferty 2018).

Minsky has a well-established reputation as a heterodox economist who sought to recover the radical impulse of Keynes' critique following its integration into mainstream economics during the early post-war period (e.g. Wray 2016). On this reading, Minsky is a critic of speculation and overindebtedness, very much along the lines of the heterodox critique of financial speculation that we have already discussed here. This is in some respects a plausible interpretation, but it is also a highly selective one that isn't able to do much with the fact that Minsky was keenly aware of the speculative nature of economic life in general (Mehrling 1999; Minsky 1996). And while it is certainly true that Minsky was predominantly concerned with the world of high finance and paid relatively little attention to the ways in which asset logics were becoming embedded in everyday life, his way of thinking is nonetheless useful for understanding that process.

It is important here to understand why exactly we should see Minsky's work as not simply rehearsing or elaborating on Keynes' original analysis but as advancing on it. Keynes relied on a particular understanding of financial speculation. In *The General Theory* (1936: 158) he famously compared its logic to that of a newspaper beauty competition, where people vote not so much on the basis of how they themselves feel but rather on the basis of what they think others think. Such speculative activity is concerned with manipulating the 'psychology' of the market, rather than 'forecasting the prospective yield of assets over their whole life', the fundamental value of things based on the production of material goods and services (p. 156). In other words, as much as he was concerned with the possibility of fluctuations in the way investors valued things, Keynes always held on to the idea of a long-run market outcome that would reflect the real value of things – as if there exists a neutral notion of what the 'whole life' of something consists in, a time of life that was simply naturally given, rather than shaped by the dynamics of capitalism. Keynes was then reluctant to accept that the logic of the newspaper beauty contest – a game of valuation driven by mutual expectations, in which people speculate on what other people are thinking and promising – was not a troubling divergence from foundational economic values but in fact the core logic of economic life.

The Minsky that has received most attention over the past decade is the one who is consistent with the Keynes who rejected speculation as a sort of ontologically incoherent or unsustainable practice. But this misses out on his most important insights: Minsky realized that all economic choices and investments were speculative in the sense that their value would only be determined in a future that is unknowable because it will be shaped by events that we cannot predict. Thus Minsky thought of debt and speculation not as pathological features of an otherwise robust capitalism based on the production of real things. Instead, he viewed the logic of debt and credit, of speculative promises and projections into the future, as the very stuff of capitalist life.

For Minsky, economic actors are essentially balance sheet entities, working on the basis of promises received and promises made (2008 [1986]). They raise cash by extending promises and they use this cash value to make investments, to buy promises made by others. At issue here was not whether the amount of debt taken on was sound in some metaphysical sense, but rather the entirely practical fact that economic actors need to generate sufficient cash flow to be able to service their debts. This is what Minsky referred to as a liquidity constraint: whatever our long-term plans, they need to include some provisions to make it to tomorrow. I may have the world's best investment opportunity, but if I have to borrow in order to buy it and the returns it generates are not enough for me to keep up with my repayment schedule (and I don't have any other sources of cash flow), I'll be forced to sell. Liquidity buys us the time we need to make our investments work out.

This insight gave Minsky a much deeper appreciation of the nature and role of liquidity: Keynes thought of the concern with liquidity as a 'fetish', simply a refusal to commit patiently to the production of real value. But Minsky thought of it as primarily a 'survival constraint' (a term that Mehrling [1999: 139] has recovered from Minsky's doctoral thesis). The idea that we can invest all our resources in the future and patiently wait for an eventual payoff is fully premised on the possibility of taking liquidity for granted. What this means is that the capitalist economy is at its core structured in terms of time – not just in the trivial sense that things take place in time and are therefore subject to change, but in the more profound sense that it makes no sense to analyse processes of change as if they are driving towards a neutral long-term state where things are organized according to some kind of true value or purpose. Time is an active force, and the logic of credit and debt cannot be seen as a mere surface-level dynamic that takes place while more fundamental processes work themselves out. For Keynes the 'meantime' mattered because, as he famously quipped, 'in the long run we are all dead'

(Keynes 1924: 80). Minsky did not have much use for the idea of such an independently given long run: in the economic game of capitalism, some survive and others die, some thrive and others languish.

The Minskyan household is usefully contrasted with the Keynesian household of the early post-war era, which functioned in a context that lent considerable credibility to the imaginary of fundamental, non-speculative value. To the extent that it participated in an asset economy of sorts, this typically involved the purchase of a home whose value was not subject to great fluctuations, and it had access to a stable (mostly male) wage that allowed it to make mortgage payments. The typical Minskyan household, by contrast, purchases a home not just with a view to paying down the mortgage but also hoping to achieve capital gains. It seeks not just returns on an investment of stable value, but it is concerned to see the asset itself appreciate in value. Nor should we think of this as an optional extra – often the anticipation of capital gains is essential to plans to finance the asset, not least because income from wages is nowadays also far more volatile than it used to be for many households. The Minskyan household is not simply under pressure to make prudent investments; in an economic system where everyone speculates, it needs to invest in assets that will become the object of others' economic self-interest and speculative investments and so will appreciate (Feher 2009).

Again, to speak of a Minskyan household, as we do, is to emphasize the insertion of the contemporary household into a speculative, future-oriented logic. The operative principle here is leverage; that is, financing investments with borrowed funds that need to be paid back. This can amplify the effects of a good investment, but it can similarly amplify the effects of a bad investment. The asset economy works on a procyclical logic: asset appreciation (i.e. balance sheet expansion) interacts in a mutually reinforcing way with the ability to borrow, leverage and make new investments. But this principle also works the other way around: asset depreciation interacts in a mutually reinforcing way with the declining ability to borrow, leverage and make new investments. As we will see, a significant source of policy leverage has to do with the ability to influence this dynamic – in particular, the possibility of kickstarting it in certain areas but not in others, and the ability to short-circuit a deflationary spiral in some areas but not in others. Much of what we think about in terms of the politics of financial regulation revolves around this. The distinctiveness of neoliberal political economy is not primarily to be found in the growing reach of a generic commodity calculus, nor in the growing influence of a liquidity paradigm; but in the way fiscal and monetary policies have produced distinctive logics of asset appreciation and depreciation (Adkins 2018; Konings 2018).

To set the stage for the rest of the story, it is important here to recognize explicitly that another word for asset appreciation is inflation, an increase in monetary value without any corresponding change in the nature of the good itself or the conditions of its production that would make it scarcer or justify an increased demand for it. Of course, the official story is that we live in a world without inflation. In most Western countries, consumer price inflation has been low and stable for several decades. But this obscures the fact that inflation elsewhere has been central to the making of the neoliberal asset economy. Of course, we tend not to think of asset price inflation as inflation, but that is itself the product of a particular historical conjuncture and discursive configuration. It is therefore important to understand the transition from the Keynesian to the neoliberal era as a shift from price inflation towards asset inflation. During the 1970s, price inflation was closely bound up with wage growth as both cause (high wage increases leads employers to offset this as much as possible by pushing up prices) and consequence (high levels of inflation lead unions to make higher wage demands), and it was increasingly perceived as threatening asset values. As we will explain in more detail in the next chapter, the neoliberal shift in policymaking reversed this dynamic.

The centrality of housing

The growth of asset prices over the past decades has been most prominently charted in Piketty's (2014) *Capital in the Twenty-First Century*. He argues that the growth of asset values has outstripped the growth of the economy in general and of wages in particular, and that this is a key factor driving growing inequalities in Western political economies. However, Piketty's analysis is strongly focused on the runaway wealth of the very top layers (the 1%) and does not pursue a more general reconsideration of class and stratification. Perhaps we should excuse an economist for not venturing into such sociological terrain; but not only has Piketty had no hesitation in wading into political and sociological debates on related issues, very few of the many social scientists who have drawn on Piketty's work have pursued the implications of his observations in a systematic way to rethink contemporary logics of class and stratification. Instead, social scientists have generally remained within the parameters of Piketty's own analysis, layering empirical observations about the growing role of asset wealth on top of a conceptual model of inequality that is still centred around employment-based categories such as wage income and occupational status.

While we are by no means concerned to deny the reality of the 1% and the fact that the present era is seeing a curious revival of conspicuous displays of opulence, the reason why we are talking of an 'economy of assets' is that such trends should be seen as part of a wider logic of asset ownership that includes a large percentage of households. This means that the story we are telling here offers a different emphasis from that offered by Piketty, who sees asset appreciation in terms of a return to the plutocracy of the gilded age.

From a certain angle, the distance from an analysis of accelerating capital accumulation and growing inequality to a theorization of class and stratification would seem to be a short one to travel. It is therefore useful to consider what it is about Piketty's framing of growing inequality that has prevented it from being translated more readily into a general theory of class and stratification. Conceptually, it is significant that Piketty's work vacillates between two images of the shift that has fostered the growth of inequality. On the one hand, it relies on a theory of natural economic laws that display inherent tendencies to wealth accumulation (expressed in the now famous formula r>g) and that can only ever be interrupted or slowed down from the outside. Insofar as such a perspective is concerned with questions of policy and institutions, it tends to emphasize the *absence* of policy interventions that might have redressed trends of growing inequality; his work is largely silent on specific institutional mechanisms of policymaking and the way these have actively constructed qualitatively new patterns of capital accumulation. On the other hand, Piketty emphasizes the ways in which large fortunes have captured the institutions of politics and governance, a plutocratic structure that blocks any attempts to reverse the inegalitarian effects of the logic of capital.

These images are not specific to Piketty's work but reflect more general tendencies to attribute the trends of recent decades to economic or political logics, or a combination of them. Even when these factors are articulated in sophisticated ways, the result is often still an analysis that portrays neoliberalism as a return to a more basic form of capitalism modelled on the experience of nineteenth-century liberalism – that is, capital as it operated before the innovations associated with the twentieth-century welfare state and the way those effected an integration of the population into the capitalist system not simply by higher wages and full employment but also through connecting them to mechanisms of saving, investment and asset building: above all property ownership (Cahill & Konings 2017). The observation that especially in Anglo-American countries the promotion of asset ownership was a key aspect of mid-twentieth-century capitalism is far from new (Chwieroth & Walter 2019); but its implications are insufficiently recognized when it comes to the analysis of class restructuring in the contemporary era. In other words, the fact that over the course of the twentieth century large segments of the population came to participate in dynamics of asset and home ownership means that the model of semi-automatic accumulation of rentier wealth in the hands of a small set of elites is of limited use when it comes to understanding the wider reconfiguration of class and inequality.

Connecting capital to class requires a more institution-based understanding of capital. Along such lines, Naidu (2017) has provided a useful perspective on the way mainstream and critical themes intertwine in Piketty's work, distinguishing between a 'domesticated Piketty' and an underdeveloped 'wild Piketty' who becomes visible only intermittently. Domesticated

Piketty relies on an understanding of capital found in the neoclassical model, which sees capital as a fund of savings and is incapable of doing justice to the specific character of capital compared to other production factors. Wild Piketty develops close affinities with the definition of capital that has been developed in the institutionalist tradition with which Minsky was closely affiliated (Mehrling 1999), which emphasizes both the political and legally constructed nature of property rights and the forward-looking, always partially speculative character of capital. From this perspective, capital is 'a forward-looking claim on future resources' (Naidu 2017: 108).

The ability to define and enforce property rights in order to secure income flows from assets is an issue that prominently involves legal, political and other institutions, and the contestations that take place inside them. As Naidu points out, in this respect, the 'rise of housing wealth is uniquely interesting, as housing and land are intrinsically tied to particular policies and local politics' (Naidu 2017: 120). Housing plays an important, if largely unacknowledged role in the story that Piketty tells. The widely publicized Rognlie (2015) paper noted this, and conservatively inclined commentators have seized on it to downplay the importance of Piketty's findings and to shift the conversation from the taxation of wealth to the way regulations create an artificial scarcity of real estate (e.g. DeVore 2015). From the perspective of our analysis, however, acknowledging the role of housing allows us to bring out the real point of Piketty's analysis more fully (Guyer 2015). That is, the significance of Piketty's results resides *precisely* in the fact that so much of the growth of wealth has been due to the growth of house prices: it demonstrates the extent to which the current phase of capitalism does not represent a return to an era of old money, haute finance and aristocratic rentiers, but involves the structural reconfiguration of patterns of inequality in a context that has seen the rise of home ownership and the growth of asset ownership across numerous layers of the population. This opens up the possibility of a closer connection to the issue of class, one that recognizes that the spread of asset ownership has created new, complex dynamics of stratification.

Of course, housing is not the only asset category that is relevant here. Most notably, the stock market has also become the object of middle-class investment (often, but not exclusively through retirement funds). During the 1980s and 1990s this was certainly the most visible and widely noted way in which asset ownership was spreading, but as a consequence the impact of stock ownership on inequality – including a significant literature on the paradoxical class positions that emerge when pension funds own stock in companies and so acquire an interest in the kind of restructuring strategies that typically are to the detriment of employees (Skerrett et al. 2017) – has already received significant attention.

The implications of the financial dynamics of housing and mortgage markets for our understanding of stratification are, however, yet to be fully pursued. But this is not simply a question of empirical focus (i.e. we are not simply filling a gap in the literature), it is also a more qualitative claim about the nature of housing as an asset. That is to say, as an asset, housing works in a distinctive way that gives it a specific role in the creation of inequality. On the one hand, almost all households participate in the housing market as either renters or owners, and the wish to own a house is often not simply driven by financial considerations but equally by cultural influences and family considerations. On the other hand, switching from renting to buying is not nearly as easy as switching savings from a bank account to a mutual fund – instead, it requires a down payment and then leveraging that by taking on debt. It is increasingly difficult for all but the highest income earners to save up a deposit through wages alone. The need for a lump-sum payment to break into the market means that intergenerational transfers of wealth come to play a central role and that the generational dimension shapes the logic of class in new ways – no longer limited to the inheritance of large fortunes but necessary also for people on relatively high wages who wish to break into an otherwise inaccessible property market. Those who can't afford the down payment are increasingly forced to put the financial flows and income streams they generate in the service of others' asset accumulation (exemplified in the phenomenon of long-term renters paying down the mortgage on a property owned by someone else).

Governing the asset economy

In this book we explore how asset inflation has reconfigured the logic of class and inequality. This implies a different emphasis (i.e. a more 'sociological' concern) from other works that have examined the growing role of property inflation from more of a 'political economy' angle, which has focused more centrally on its macroeconomic effects and the instability it has engendered (Aalbers & Christophers 2014; Fuller 2019; Keen 2017; Schwartz & Seabrooke 2009; Weber 2015). Crucially, however, these aspects cannot be separated and the task we set ourselves is to articulate how they combine: bringing the sociological dimension more into the centre of the analysis will allow us to connect these two aspects in ways that will improve our understanding of them in their interconnection. In particular, we advance on existing political economy interpretations in two ways.

First, the political economy critique typically places a heavy emphasis on the unsustainable character of property inflation – that is, the idea that the growth of asset values is not supported by economic fundamentals and that this means that the bubble must sooner or later burst. Commentary on the state of the housing market has often assumed the form of 'what goes up, must come down'. It is, however, important to appreciate the relatively sustained nature of property inflation. At different points in the past decades commentators have declared the collapse of the housing market, but this has yet to take place. The financial crisis of 2007–8 was widely expected to put a stop to several decades of credit growth and property inflation, but failed to do so. Indeed, the rise in house prices has been particularly pronounced since then.

It is entirely true that in an important sense rising real estate valuations are purely speculative – that is, reflecting not fundamentals but what people think others will be willing to pay for real estate in the future. Indeed, in a key respect the housing market is speculative in a particularly transparent way. When it comes to a rising stock market, there may be considerable confusion about whether or not price increases make sense because the degree to which the nature of underlying assets is itself changing is often extremely unclear. In the case of real estate, by contrast, it is apparent that the underlying asset isn't changing much – that is to say, there is little innovation taking place in the property industry, and as a consequence is it very apparent to buyers themselves that their willingness to buy at a certain price is bound up not with any beliefs about true underlying values but about the future of market sentiment and expectations about what others will be willing to pay.

And yet, despite this element of transparency (which one might expect would amplify even minor shocks into full-blown meltdowns), property markets in large urban centres have been remarkably resilient. This indicates that an upward momentum has been built into the market: property inflation is produced by, and now anchored in, a particular institutional configuration of path-dependent public policymaking and the expectations that it fosters. Homeowners are provided with benefits and protection from risk that work to prevent market slumps from developing into meltdowns. Even though downturns in the property market do occur all the time, they often resemble momentary setbacks or temporary plateaus rather than full-on crashes. This logic whereby policies put a floor under the market is most spectacularly evident when authorities step in to bail out a large financial institution about to fail. But spectacular bailouts are only the tip of the iceberg, as Minsky realized: risk-shifting through fiscal and monetary policy mechanisms is an integral part of the way in which an asset-driven economic system functions. It works to support the balance sheets of actors that are systematically important in both a political and economic sense.

Second, when critical political economy scholarship is more attuned to the specific institutional sources of asset inflation and the way this is maintained by specific policies, it has difficulty comprehending why the problems that it highlights seem so intractable, and why the pro-asset inflation orientation of policymaking seems locked in place despite growing awareness of the problems it creates. This pertains to the negative distributional effects of the asset economy (the very logic of fuelling asset inflation means that it becomes harder and harder for people to buy into these logics) as well as the fact that the asset-driven character of economic growth has entered a phase of diminishing returns. With each round of financial stimulus (such as quantitative easing), more asset inflation is needed to achieve a given increase in growth and employment. Political economy scholars typically have a great deal of difficulty understanding why public policy seems unable to shift away from policies promoting asset inflation despite growing awareness of its destabilizing effects.

It is telling that such an otherwise politically middle-of-the-road scholar as Piketty stresses the growth of a plutocracy, the concentration of public authority in the wealthiest. This is an increasingly common move: 'capture theory' and instrumentalist understandings of institutional power have migrated from explicitly right-wing and left-wing theory to respectable social science (Brink & Teles 2017; Manish & O'Reilly 2019; McCarty 2013). But it remains more description than explanation. Economic elites always have more influence on public institutions, but if policy is fully captured in a way that appears increasingly irrational to everyone involved, we need an explanation of how such capture can persist in a democratic society. Key here is an appreciation of the role that housing has played in the creation of a middle class that is often seen as the backbone of social stability and that politicians and policymakers are reluctant to alienate. Neoliberal policies occurred in a historical and institutional setting where property ownership was already significantly democratized, and they were at least initially successful in building on that legacy. This has created a specific middle-class constituency that is deeply invested in the promise of asset appreciation, and it is in this context that we should understand the fact that a pro-asset inflation policy orientation has become locked in.

The Making of the Asset Economy

Price inflation and asset deflation in the 1970s

The key 'data point' on which the argument of this book turns is the long-term divergence of wages and asset values, in particular property prices. It is therefore important to acknowledge that the combination of inflating asset prices and stagnant wages does not represent a natural tendency to which capitalism reverts when extraneous regulations have been removed. Rather, strenuous institutional efforts were required to create this state of affairs. During the 1970s, precisely the opposite dynamic – asset price stagnation in combination with wage and consumer price inflation – had come to prevail. The combination of unemployment along with high wages and consumer price inflation signalled the practical limits of Keynesianism as a mode of governance. The wage and consumer price spiral of the 1970s was the symptom of an undecided struggle between different social groups who sought to maintain their respective shares of the national income at a time when economic growth was faltering. Unionized workers secured wage gains that matched and often outpaced the simultaneous efforts of employers to push up consumer prices. In the US, steel workers held their own against management as they forced wages to rise faster than the cost of living (Hoerr 1988). In the UK, trade unions chafed against the limits of then Labour Prime Minister James Callaghan's wage controls until, during the Winter of Discontent of 1978–9, a wave of wildcat strikes brought the nation to a standstill and workers pushed through wage increases well in excess of the consumer price index (Medhurst 2014; Shepherd 2016). In Australia too, government efforts to index wages fell foul of a restive labour movement in the late 1970s (Kaufman 2004: 427). While employers had traditionally used the threat of unemployment to break the back of labour, this was no longer feasible at a time when unemployment benefits were generous enough to live on and welfare benefits were often indexed to inflation.

In the United States, since wages and welfare for the most part kept pace with the consumer price index, the lower and middle classes did not lose much through inflation, and in some cases they made considerable gains (Minarik 1980: 225–77). Those who benefited most from inflation were the middle-income homeowners who had borrowed to buy a house. With fixed mortgage repayments and interest rates, indebted homeowners saw their mortgage burden depreciate in value (p. 228). Even renters were not overly burdened by inflation, as wages tended to keep up with rent increments. The effect of rising consumer prices on welfare recipients was offset by the fact that most welfare programmes were adjusted to inflation (p. 226). Nor did inflation increase the tax burden on the American poor and middle class, as right-wing commentators have often argued. The impact of inflation-induced bracket creep on the taxes of low- and middle-income workers was neutralized by the introduction of a series of personal exemptions and deductions during the same period (Hibbs 1987: 90–2). For lower-income groups, effective income tax rates actually fell between 1970 and 1979, making the entire income tax system more progressive (p. 92).

By contrast, inflation seriously eroded the wealth of the top decile and centile of households – those whose wealth was invested in financial assets such as stocks, bonds, or Treasury bills and whose income derived primarily from interests, dividends, rents and capital gains. Throughout the 1970s, wealth holders were at a loss to find safe avenues of investment that would protect their assets from depreciation. The real value of corporate stock had been falling steadily since the mid-1960s, while bondholders found themselves earning low, if not negative, real interest rates (Minarik 1980: 228). As inflation kept spiralling upward, major uncertainty surrounded the future of long-term investments such as Treasury bonds. Wage and consumer price inflation thus translated into asset deflation (Konings 2009; Phillips 2003).

Shifts in the tax and financial regime

Although the threat to asset prices was felt throughout the world of Anglo-American finance (Epstein & Jayadev 2005; Jordà et al. 2019), the issue of asset depreciation became particularly vexed in the United States. This was the case in large part because during the same period capital gains and investment income were also coming under attack from progressive tax reformers. In the early 1970s, Democratic candidate

George McGovern promised a radical redistribution of wealth via the tax code (Silk 1972), and many of the same ideas were taken up by Jimmy Carter later in the decade (Graetz 1976). During his 1976 campaign, Carter promised to equalize the taxation of capital gains and ordinary income and called for the tax code to be more progressive. The overarching objective of his reforms was to shift the weight of the tax burden from low- and middle-income earners, who received few of the advantages of the capital gains tax, to high-income earners, who were overwhelmingly the beneficiaries of asset price gains (Bartlett 2013).

A Wall Street-driven counter-offensive sprang into existence to contest Carter's proposals. Rallying to their cause, a number of high-profile economists sought to demonstrate why the taxation of capital gains as ordinary income would be disastrous for the American economy. Martin Feldstein in particular was a formidable opponent of Carter's progressive tax reforms. During his time as president of the prestigious National Bureau for Economic Research, Feldstein published a series of influential studies claiming to show that increases in the capital gains tax stifled new business investment, diminished government revenues and froze the asset market by locking investors into existing asset positions (Feldstein 1978; Feldstein & Slemrod 1978). Emanating from the most prestigious quarters of academia, Feldstein's ideas were applauded and popularized by a new cadre of supply-side economists, who argued that tax incentives to investment were the surest way of stimulating economic growth and replenishing government coffers without causing inflation (Domitrovic 2012).

The campaign was highly effective and the tax reform bill that Carter eventually presented was considerably diluted (Kuttner 1980: 242). Not satisfied with this partial victory, Carter's opponents pushed for an alternative bill that would further diminish the existing tax burden on capital gains. The Revenue Act of 1978 was highly regressive: the tax savings it generated overwhelmingly benefited the wealthiest households (p. 247). But the legislation received a popular sanction of sorts from middle-income homeowners in California, who were fighting their own battle against taxation on their appreciated housing wealth. As noted by Michelmore (2012: 128), 'the Revenue Act of 1978, the last tax bill of the decade, provided a dress rehearsal for the tax politics of the Reagan era'.

As part of his tax cuts programme of 1981, Reagan slashed the maximum capital gains rate to only 20%, restoring it to its lowest level since the Hoover administration, and raised the exemption threshold on estate tax (Phillips 1990: 76–8). In 1986, however, budget pressures forced Reagan to reverse course and equalize the tax treatment of capital gains and ordinary income (although, in practice, the maximum capital gains tax increased only slightly, since the top rates of ordinary income had also been subject to steep cuts in the meantime). But this decision was again overturned by George W Bush, who in 2003 lowered the top tax on capital gains to 15% and introduced lower rates for dividends. Trump increased the estate tax exemption in 2017 and is currently trying to push through a further reduction to the capital gains tax. As a consequence of these changes to the tax code, capital gains and investment income are currently taxed at a much lower rate than income from labour, with predictable effects on the overall distribution of wealth and income.

Supply-side arguments in favour of preferential taxation of capital gains have also been exported to other countries. In Australia, the Labor government of Prime Minister Bob Hawke introduced a capital gains tax for the first time in 1985 as part of its project to fashion a more equitable tax system (Head 1990). But this project was watered down, first by Labor Prime Minister Paul Keating's 1987 decision to allow so-called 'negative gearing' or tax concessions for overleveraged investments, and more resoundingly by Liberal Prime Minister John Howard's sweeping cuts to capital gains tax, in 1999. Howard's tax reforms were directly inspired by the American supply-sider Alan Reynolds, who had been commissioned by the Australian Stock Exchange to report on incentives to investment (Review of Business Taxation 1999; Reynolds 1999; *Sydney Morning Herald* 2004). The decision to introduce preferential tax treatment for capital gains was sold as an incentive to stock market investment and innovation, but served, more prosaically, as a boost to the market in housing investment in Australia (Quiggin 2004). Negative gearing has long served as a lucrative tax shelter for wage and salary earners on a high marginal tax rate, since Australia is one of the few countries in which losses can be claimed against *any* source of income, including income from labour (Daley & Wood 2014). But until Howard's tax reforms, negative gearing only allowed investors to *postpone* their income tax burden to the moment of sale, when they would become fully liable for capital gains tax, calculated at an individual's highest marginal tax rate. When Howard halved the capital gains tax for investments, negative gearing became much more attractive since it was no longer simply a means of deferring income taxes but of permanently reducing them (Eslake 2013: 9). The combined effect of such incentives is to allow investors to convert income from labour into income from capital at will – thereby halving their marginal tax rates (Daley & Wood 2014: 17). Thus, in a context where government policy is otherwise actively seeking to moderate wages, negative gearing has allowed high earners and investors to exempt themselves from the progressive taxation of both their investment and labour income (Atkinson & Leigh 2007).

In the UK also, supply-side prescriptions have ushered in a more regressive tax regime, characterized by a generalized reduction in income taxes alongside an increase in consumption taxes, whose costs are borne disproportionately by low-income wage earners. In his 1988 budget, then Chancellor of the Exchequer Nigel Lawson slashed the top rate of income tax (including both income from labour and capital) to 40%. While this reform equalized the taxation of wages and capital gains, Lawson simultaneously introduced a back-door sweetener to asset holders by amending the capital gains tax to correct for losses from consumer price inflation (Healey 1992). In the 2008 Budget, the Labour government of Gordon Brown undertook a much more radical round of supply-side reforms when it introduced a new single capital gains rate of 18% and put an end to 'taper relief' provisions which had been designed to reward longer-term investment in business assets (Seely 2010). The abolition of taper relief was designed to stop the widespread abuse of such provisions by private equity firms. And yet the progressive impact of the reform was offset by an unprecedented cut to the general rate of capital gains taxation. In defence of these changes, Chancellor of the Exchequer Alistair Darling boasted that 'we want to reward investment' so 'we are right to now tax gains at a lower rate than income – and the new single rate is among the most competitive in the world, is less than half the top rate for income, and is also less than half what it was ten years ago' (Darling 2007).

As in Australia, the impact of such tax concessions has been particularly pronounced when it comes to housing. The introduction of the capital gains tax in 1965 was accompanied by an exemption for primary residences, a concession that made some sense at a time when house prices were on a par with wage and consumer price inflation and the private housing market was closely integrated with the council housing sector. But as private housing and rentals have come to dominate the sector, the capital gains exemption has helped fuel the transformation of residential housing into a lucrative financial asset, unburdened by the tax rates that accrue to labour income (Ryan-Collins et al. 2017).

Tax reform was by no means the only institutional intervention required to reverse the wage inflation of the 1970s. What was needed was a new formula for fiscal and monetary policy that would ensure the permanence of low wages and inflated capital gains. This formula would settle into place in the 1990s, as governments and central banks agreed to collaborate on a programme of regressive taxes, 'balanced budgets' (ensuring low levels of public spending), permanent vigilance with regard to (wage and price) inflation, and a strategy of benign neglect vis-a-vis asset price inflation (Palley 2012).

Before this regime could be established, it was necessary to defeat the labour movement more decisively. In the US and the UK, the Federal Reserve and the Bank of England drove up interest rates with the objective of creating a recession. Here, Milton Friedman's 'monetarism' served as a technical pretext for the deliberate creation of a recession. Long months of unemployment brought the labour movement to its knees as governments simultaneously went to work undoing the legal and social protections of the previous decades. The bargaining power of unionized labour broken, corporations were now free to move production units offshore and cut wages to domestic workers, while the high interest rates that were maintained throughout the early 1980s brought cheap imports flooding in, putting an end to rising consumer prices. By 1982, the Federal Reserve and Bank of England appeared to have defeated wage and consumer price inflation.

In Australia, the counter-offensive came later and was less easily recognized for what it was, given the prior history of corporatist consensus-building between the trade unions and a Third Way Labor government (Humphrys 2019; Humphrys & Cahill 2017). When in 1991 the Reserve Bank of Australia sought to soften a frothy stock market by raising short-term interest rates, Paul Keating took advantage of the recession to put a final break on wage-push inflation. Invoking the need to 'snap the stick of inflation', Keating referred to high unemployment rates as the 'recession we had to have' (Bell 2004: 58–79). In the midst of the recession, a more radical measure to keep a lid on wage inflation was introduced: centralized wage bargaining was gradually phased out in favour of enterprise wage bargaining, an institutional measure that greatly undermined the negotiating powers of the trade unions (Bell & Keating 2018: 63).

During the 1990s, the new monetary orthodoxy of central bank independence and inflation targeting steadily gained ground around the world (Pixley et al. 2013). While consumer price inflation was to be suppressed at any cost, asset prices were never the target of central bank moderation strategies (Krippner 2011). Since the 1980s, central banks have come to tolerate and even encourage asset inflation, at the same time as they have been intensely vigilant about wage-push inflation (Goodhart 2001). Throughout the post-war period, wage and price inflation had been understood as benign trade-offs to full employment – a common-sense understanding that was encapsulated in the so-called Phillips curve. The monetary shocks of the early neoliberal era overturned this consensus and gradually gave rise to a new understanding of the central bank as a guardian of price stability. Central banks were now expected to demonstrate their independence from politics by steadfastly disciplining price inflation and wage growth. Under the new monetary regime, central banks spoke directly to the sensibilities of bondholders and sought to maintain their confidence by actively disciplining the policy choices of the state. If central banks had once sacrificed the value of assets to permit wage growth, they now strove to repress wages and consumer prices in the service of asset price appreciation.

To be sure, for a significant period of time, financial authorities remained concerned that asset inflation could eventually spill over into consumer price inflation, and in particular that the bailout of large financial institutions would end up having the same inflationary effects that social protections were seen to have had during the 1970s. But bailouts were, by their very nature, much more selective than the across-the-board socialization of risk of the 1970s. It took financial authorities until the 1990s to fully recognize the contours of and the possibilities opened up by this new regime. What was once seen as a major source of moral hazard – the creation of expectations of financial assistance – was increasingly treated as a policy instrument. Under Alan Greenspan's tenure as Chair of the US Federal Reserve there emerged something like a pre-emptive bailout regime, dedicated to alleviating the liquidity pressures on large institutions whenever asset prices threatened to lose their upward momentum (the 'Greenspan put'). This is entirely at odds with the classic lender-of-last-resort doctrine, which viewed central bank assistance as precisely that – a last-resort option that should only be activated after all else had failed. In this way, a regressive bias was built into the logic of asset appreciation that was critical to its continuation.

The overall effect of neoliberal monetary policy has been to reverse the relationship between wage and asset inflation that prevailed throughout the post-war era right up into the 1970s. Since the 1980s, wages have struggled to keep pace with low levels of consumer price inflation while the asset holdings of the richest households rapidly grew in value (Canterbery 2000; Greider 1989). Together, these asset price booms generated massive growth in capital gains and investment income. Wolff (1993; see also Wolff 2014) attributes much of the wealth concentration of the 1980s and beyond to the appreciation of existing stocks of wealth – that is, to capital gains on assets acquired in the past – while observing that those who derived income from labour could not hope to accumulate comparable levels of wealth from stagnant or depreciating wages (Wolff 1993: 28). Similar results have been found for the UK (Roberts et al. 2018) and Australia (Davidson et al. 2018). The result of this combined dynamic of asset appreciation and wage stagnation was to accentuate the divide between those who earned income from labour and those who derived income from capital.

Asset democratization and its contradictions

These dynamics would very likely have generated signif-icant social unrest had they not been accompanied by the promise that the gains on asset appreciation would be distributed among the wider population. The supply-side doctrine of trickle-down economics was only the crudest expression of an ideology of democratized capital that was integral to the entire project of neoliberal capitalism: governments encouraged people to participate in the asset economy to compensate for their losses on labour income with investment income. Margaret Thatcher was the first to understand the emotional appeal of that prospect when, in the midst of her attacks on unions and the public sector, she offered working-class residents the opportunity to buy their public housing assets on long-term right-to-buy schemes. This, it was hoped, would serve as a literal buy-in to the psychology of investment and encourage former dependants on the public sector to see themselves as asset holders and rentiers rather than workers.

In 1988, then Chancellor of the Exchequer Nigel Lawson foresaw a not-too-distant future when the UK would be 'a nation of inheritors', and when even working-class households would see their interests aligned with the rentier class (Hamnett 1999). In the US, Ronald Reagan touted pension fund capitalism as the trade-off for growing job insecurity and precarious wages: as workers lost their workplace protections, including defined benefit pensions, they were reassured that they could benefit from a soaring stock market via their pension plans (Davis 2009). In Australia, as the 1980s Accord between the trade unions and government became more about moderating wages than increasing the social wage, Paul Keating sought to wean workers off the wage pension by promoting the virtues of pension-fund capitalism and generalizing access to superannuation (Humphrys 2019: 148–52).

In the 1990s, Third Way policy advisors took the promise of democratized capital gains one step further when they proposed that welfare recipients too might achieve upward mobility if they could be taught how to acquire and cultivate assets (Sherraden 2005). As stock markets fizzled in the early 2000s and dreams of pension-fund capitalism faded along with them, governments across the Anglo-American world redoubled their efforts to push the wage- and welfare-poor into home ownership. The rapid expansion of a sub-prime mortgage market in the US, which allowed households on precarious and meagre incomes to buy into asset ownership by taking on extraordinary levels of debt, underscored the crucial role of cheap and abundant credit in sustaining the dream of democratized asset ownership. Only at the price of unprecedented levels of household debt did the wage-poor have any chance of earning income from assets.

Perhaps the most ambitious legacy of Third Way neoliberalism, and one that enjoyed considerable popularity at the peak of the 1990s 'new economy', was the idea that high-skilled knowledge workers and other representatives of the creative class could monetize their educational assets in the same way as investors leveraged their capital assets. The idea that wage workers might be transformed into investors through conversion of their labour power into a stock of capital has a long-standing pedigree in Chicago School human capital theory. But specific to the Third Way take on human capital is the conviction that the state must play an active role in stimulating and democratizing such assets in the first place. Championed by New Democrats and New Labour alike, the Third Way take on human capital theory sought to remedy the social fallout from generalized wage stagnation by helping all who would help themselves to convert income from high-skilled labour into income from capital. The real difference between this and other iterations of the asset-owning democracy was its attempt to reconcile meritocracy with capital gains: if homeowner democracy rewarded people for the mere fact of owning a home, and shareholder capitalism delivered returns to those who owned stock, Third Way human capital theory promised to convert genuine skill and talent into capital gains. For champions of the new economy, the asset holder was also an inventor and creator. In apparent defiance of the age-old idea that rent represents 'unearned income', capital gains would accrue to those who 'earned' them.

This version of Third Way rhetoric was particularly resonant in the US, where Clinton and his labour advisor Robert Reich were touting investment in the new high-tech economy of Silicon Valley as an alternative to the moribund manufacturing jobs of the past, and where a combination of skyrocketing stock prices and changes to the capital gains tax made stock options a major source of income growth for high-tech workers (Henwood 2003). The stock option had emerged as a form of executive payment in the 1930s, at a time when the preferential taxation of capital gains income made it much more attractive than a wage salary (Lazonick 2009: 48). It was subsequently shut down as an alternative income stream in the 1960s and rendered obsolete when the tax treatment of capital gains and ordinary income was equalized in the 1970s. But the stock option was resuscitated by the Reagan administration in 1981 when it restored the concessional tax treatment of capital gains and relaxed the rules on issuing options to employees (p. 50). The idea that IT workers and other 'symbolic analysts' would earn part of their income in the form of stock options was particularly appealing to Third Way democrats because it suggested such a literal translation of human capital.

Clinton's first Secretary of Labor, Robert Reich, was particularly influential in spreading the idea that the Fordist model of mass industrial production and unionized labour could not be salvaged and that national economies would need to adapt themselves to the realities of a new information economy in which knowledge had become the principal source of value. As production chains and financial markets become increasingly globalized, Reich argued, human capital was the only resource that a nation could claim as its own and the only drawcard that could reliably be used to attract and retain volatile investment funds (Reich 1991). National prosperity and high wages could no longer be ensured by a contract among the state, capital and trade unions: it could be secured only through the ability of national economies to attract global investment funds. The state, however, still had a role to play here in rendering its innovation regime as attractive as possible, through steady public investment in research, education and infrastructure.

Clinton's initial human capital agenda was ambitious, pledging to channel large amounts into research and development, boost federal infrastructure investment and establish a public venture capital agency to stimulate high-risk innovation (Cebul 2019: 160). In his inaugural address on 20 January 1993, Clinton announced his intention to 'create millions of long-term, good-paying jobs' through 'a program to jumpstart our economy'. The New Democrats' economic plan, titled 'Technology for America's Economic Growth: A New Direction to Build Economic Strength', foresaw public 'investments where they'll do the most good: incentives to business to create new jobs; investments in education and training' (p. 161). Cebul (2019) aptly refers to the human capital strategies of New Democrats as 'supply side liberalism': after a decade of private-capital friendly supply-side neoliberalism on the part of the Republicans and the apparent triumph of right-wing populism among the white working class, the New Democrats were convinced that demand-side interventions were doomed to political and economic failure and now argued that economic redistribution was in any case best achieved through government incentives to private investment and job creation. Their arguments differed from those of Reagan-era supply-siders only insofar as they saw government investment as a necessary stimulus to continuing growth on the supply side.

From the beginning, however, this agenda was accompanied by a commitment to public austerity, through which the New Democrats sought to differentiate themselves from their 'tax and spend' predecessors. Deficit reduction progressively took centre stage, and Clinton's more hawkish advisors, chief among them Robert Rubin, warned of the political fallout if decisive action wasn't taken (Schuldes 2011: 34–5). This, combined with the counsels of the Chair of the Federal Reserve, Alan Greenspan, who saw balanced budgets as a necessary (not simply strategic) counterpart to asset inflation, eventually overcame the modest element of centrist utopianism of Clinton's original plans. As Cebul notes, when its aspirations to fund a Third Way human capital agenda were denied, 'the Clinton administration's political imagination contained little more than reverence for entrepreneurs, high-tech sectors and a reflexive veneration of the market as the essential underwriter of market progress' (2019: 164). Clinton offered unparalleled support to private high-tech investors by strengthening worldwide protection of US intellectual property rights, and in 1997 introduced a further reduction to the capital gains tax, earning him the grudging respect of Reagan-era supply-siders (not for nothing, veteran supply-sider Arthur Laffer boasted of voting for Clinton twice in a row) (Laffer et al. 2009).

That Clinton was unable to reconcile the imperatives of fiscal conservatism with an expanded remit for state investment in human capital points to a structural contradiction at the very heart of the idea of democratized asset inflation. As Greenspan took pains to explain to Clinton, it was simply not possible to square the tremendous 'wealth effect' generated by sustained asset inflation with a programme of serious public investment. As soon as bondholders got wind of any attempt on the part of government to inflate wages or welfare, they would fear a return to the dark years of the 1970s and immediately demand an 'inflation premium' in the form of high interest rates (Woodward 1994). If it wanted to channel money into the public sector and run the risk of higher wages, the government would be putting a dampener on asset prices and capital gains. It was one thing or the other: high asset prices or public sector abundance.

Greenspan's (wage) inflation-averse monetary policy taught that the only real pathway to 'democratization' was to invite workers to purchase their own way into the asset economy, by taking on ever-greater levels of private consumer credit. Not everyone began life with the same stock of assets, contrary to the gospel of Chicago School human capital theory. But everyone could borrow their way into the asset economy with the help of unusually cheap and abundant credit. By deferring the moment of reckoning and offering consumer credit on historically unprecedented terms, Greenspan's credit-contingent version of democratized asset ownership offered a distant second best to Clinton's public investment pathway. As long as the government took advantage of this credit boom to push the income-poor to invest in housing, a virtuous circle would materialize whereby cheap credit would push up housing prices which would in turn provide ever-appreciating collateral for the extension of further credit. Rather than return to a discredited politics of social investment and wage growth, an option that would in any case be blocked at every turn by the Federal Reserve, Greenspan urged Clinton to generalize the 'wealth effect' of asset appreciation by relaxing the rules on credit (Greenspan 2002).

Third Way governments have typically followed this path, namely beginning by touting the virtues of the knowledge economy and ending up reverting to housing or stocks as the most practical route to policy change. Ultimately, it is impossible to create a new middle class of highly paid knowledge workers while at the same time enacting the rule of generalized wage suppression and public spending austerity. It is private housing that has allowed governments to go furthest with the promise of asset democratization because housing is the asset that is already most widely shared among a broad segment of the population. The enduring catastrophe of the global financial crisis stems from the fact that it complicated what had long seemed the easiest route to asset-based democracy – upward mobility through home ownership. In recent years, it has become clear that private housing has itself come to serve as a major generator of inequality.

The initial success of home ownership democratization policies stemmed from the fact that they could build on the accumulated legacy of post-war housing policies, which through direct public investment in council housing (the UK), subsidies to consumer credit (the US) or some combination thereof (Australia) managed to durably raise levels of private home tenure without generating house price inflation in excess of wages. These pre-existing conditions made it relatively easy for governments in the 1980s and 1990s to usher in a new cohort of homeowners. All it required was to coax renters – and in some cases, welfare recipients – to take out government-subsidized loans (the US and Australia) or convert their council housing tenure into private property through right-to-buy schemes (the UK), while at the same time introducing policies to convert housing into an investment asset. Once this first cohort of former working-class citizens had been leveraged into asset ownership (with real shifts in class position – the transition from renter or public housing resident to homeowner has turned many a former dependant of the public sector into a small-time fiscal conservative), the price of entry has become increasingly prohibitive and the promise of democratization ever more distant. The combination of inflated capital gains and deflated wages progressively closes the gates to newcomers, who struggle to buy their way into housing on wages alone. The solution of cheap consumer credit also starts to reach its limits when growing numbers of retirees find themselves using their pensions or borrowing from children to service mortgages.

Nor surprisingly then, in each of the countries we have been looking at, home ownership rates have been going backwards over the past decade, in defiance of all government efforts at democratization (Cribb et al. 2018; La Cava et al. 2017; US Census Bureau 2019). This is most visible among younger generations, but the trend is now also discernible among older cohorts, which means that the ranks of lifelong renters are growing and absolute lifetime rates of home ownership have fallen. As wages have continued to stagnate, existing wealth inequalities are being consolidated and accentuated. We have moved then from a brief period of relative wealth democratization (with some sectors of the former working class making real class shifts) to a period of lock-in, where social mobility is freezing and the bridge between homeowners and renters is closing.

Taken together, these trends open up the possibility that, if current policy conditions remain the same, access to housing wealth will become ever more concentrated and ever more dependent on family wealth. Average wage earners who, three or four decades ago, may have been able to enter the housing market by saving up for a deposit, are now increasingly reliant on intergenerational transfers to make their first leap into home ownership (Barrett et al. 2015a, 2015b; Christophers 2018; Flynn & Schwartz 2017; Ronald & Lennartz 2018). The ramifications extend far beyond the question of housing, given the now central role played by housing in financing all kinds of human services that were once funded by the state. The possibility of pursuing a tertiary education or the compulsory unpaid internship now very often requires monetary or in-kind support from family in the form of rental assistance, rent-free shared housing, or parents acting as loan guarantors or taking on student debt on behalf of adult children (Cooper 2017; Oliver et al. 2016; Zaloom 2019). Not only does housing wealth beget housing wealth, progressively narrowing the pool of those able to enter the housing market, it also increasingly determines one's educational opportunities and hence one's future earning potential and professional status. The escalation of house prices in major cities around the world has carved deep chasms of inequality between classes of people who earn the same wages but are differentiated by their status as homeowners or renters. Where once we might have placed these people in the same 'class' based on the kind of work they did, today it is obvious that these people belong to different echelons of the social scale. In such an environment, class can no longer realistically be identified as a simple function of wages from labour (working, middle and upper class) or professional status (blue collar, white collar, pink collar) and must instead be rethought in terms of asset ownership.

New Class Realities

Lineages of class theory

In the previous chapter we emphasized the growing disjunction between the promises and the accomplishments of the project of democratized asset ownership. In this chapter we will take a closer look at the specific logics of inequality that the rise of the asset economy has produced. Although the phenomenon of property inflation has received plenty of commentary, when it comes to thinking about class, inequality and stratification in more systematic ways we often tend to revert to older models based on work and occupation. Every city-dweller, including many researchers living in large cities, knows that the logic of property prices, and whether one is 'in' or 'out' of the market, has a massive impact on one's socio-economic situation – that it has fundamentally restructured how people's lives are organized and lived. But when those same people start thinking about class and inequality, they find themselves drawn to an employment-centred model that abstracts from this very fact. This chapter analyses that changing logic of stratification. We ask how exactly we should trace the distributive effects of the twin logics of asset appreciation and wage depreciation.

The significance of our argument about the importance of asset ownership for an understanding of class needs to be seen against the fact that class has conventionally been understood first and foremost with reference to work and employment. From the 1970s onwards, both broadly Marxist and broadly Weberian perspectives have elaborated this basic idea in detailed ways.

Marxist and neo-Marxists have developed elaborate class schemes focusing on the antagonistic relationship between owners and employers on the one hand and waged workers/employees on the other, as well as on the ambiguity associated with the self-employed and the managerial and supervisory occupations that expanded in the post-World War Two era. Erik Olin Wright, for example, proposed a six-point (1978, 1979), and then a revised twelve-point (1985, 1997, 1998 [1989]) class scheme along such lines. In his twelve-point scheme, class positions ranged from the bourgeoisie at one end to the proletariat at the other, with ten intermediate classes. Wright understood these intermediate classes as sitting in a complex set of relations to each other and, in the context of the growth of white-collar jobs, included semi-credentialled workers, uncredentialled supervisors, expert managers and small employers. Despite this complexity, at its core, positions in Wright's scheme depended on relationships to the means of production, and especially the abilities of classes relative to each other to extract surplus value from labour.

While Marxist and neo-Marxist class schemes focused on the antagonism between employers and employees or between capital and labour, the model of class developed in the post-war period that has unambiguously been the most influential has been the functionalist scheme developed by John Goldthorpe and colleagues at Nuffield College, Oxford. This scheme – sometimes referred to as the Nuffield class schema – rejects the emphasis on the owner–worker dynamic found in classifications such as Wright's, and instead emphasizes the differentiation of labour in advanced industrial societies (Goldthorpe & Marshall 1992). This differentiation is seen as related to the proliferation of administrative and managerial functions associated with the rise of corporate and bureaucratic organizations in advanced industrial societies. For Goldthorpe and his colleagues, such processes – including the transformations of property into corporate forms and the bureaucratization of labour and organizations – produce a class structure whereby the social position of actors is constituted in employment relations – that is, in their occupational position.

In large part because of its functionalism and scientism, and by providing a class scheme that could be effectively operationalized by using measures of occupational and employment positions (see Savage 2016), the Nuffield class schema has been the most successful and influential classificatory class scheme (see Crompton 2008; Savage et al. 2013). Most notably, in 2000 it became the UK government's official measure of class in the form of the National Statistics Socio-Economic Classification (NS-SEC). In addition, a Europe-wide classification – the European Socio-economic Classification (ESeC) – based on the Nuffield schema has recently been initiated (Rose & Harrison 2011). As this suggests, one of the key virtues of the schema is that its operationalization has allowed the generation of comparable datasets across different national domains. Such comparisons were previously not possible given the predominance of nationally specific class measurement schemes.

In their writings, Goldthorpe and his colleagues were at pains to highlight the difference between the Nuffield schema and its Marxist and post-Marxist counterparts (see, for example, Goldthorpe & Marshall 1992). They nevertheless viewed the social position of actors as constituted through employment relations and occupational positions. It is, then, crucial to recognize that the competing schemes shared the view that work, employment and the employment relationship were the key drivers in the constitution of class positions. Indeed, this view remains social science orthodoxy (see, for example, Connelly et al. 2016; Lambert & Bihagen 2014; McGovern et al. 2007).

That is not to say that the employment view of class has gone uncontested. One of the more significant developments in class theory to have strained against employment-based class schemes was the broadening of the term 'capital' in sociological theory under the influence of Pierre Bourdieu's work. This work emphasizes the role that different forms (economic, cultural and social) of capital played in the constitution of class. It was initially anchored in innovative qualitative studies (see, for example, Reay 1998; Skeggs 1997), and over time generated larger scale studies based on national surveys that analysed how stocks of different capital interact to produce class positions (see, for example, Bennett et al. 1999; Lamont 1992). The Cultural Capital and Social Exclusion project in the UK, for example, designed by Mike Savage and colleagues, explored the social, cultural and economic dimensions of class, and involved a national sample survey (Bennett et al. 2009). It found that while clear class boundaries in the structure of cultural tastes existed, 'key class boundaries were not the same as those identified in the Nuffield class schema' (Savage 2016: 68). As Savage put it, these findings 'opened the way for Bourdieusian perspectives to more directly engage with Goldthorpe's model of class' (p. 68). They led, for example, to the high-profile Great British Class Survey (GBCS), which developed a new model of class for contemporary Britain (Savage et al. 2013, 2015), and was subsequently replicated in Australia (Sheppard & Biddle 2017). This survey established a seven-point class scheme (from the elite to the precariat) where class positions are grounded not only in occupations but in economic capital more broadly stated (including household income, household savings and house price), as well as in cultural and social capital. The key finding of this survey was that the British class structure had changed such that the conventional fixation on the boundary between middle and working classes in class analysis 'should be replaced by a greater focus on the elite at the top of the social structure, the precariat at the bottom, and a more complex range of classes in the middle ranges' (Savage 2016: 68).

While the opening up of the role of capital in the GBCS to include assets is certainly to be welcomed, there is a sense in which it is too little, too late. It is not able to do justice to the significance of asset holdings in shaping class positions, in part because of continued reliance on the assumption that class status is determined in the last instance by employment position, and in part because of a preoccupation with the role of symbolic and cultural forms of capital at the expense of attention to economic and financial capital. Thus, although the GBCS pays attention to house value and total household income over and above wages, it nonetheless fails to distinguish between sources of income (income from labour or wages versus income from assets such as rents, dividends, interest and capital gains), and asset ownership does not operate as a key variable in the final list of class categories. This has the effect of obscuring the growing relative importance of asset ownership in the shaping of class positions and determining the source of one's income.

A more significant challenge to the assumed centrality of employment in the determination of class has come from authors working in heterodox political economy, who have focused on the emergence of indebtedness as a necessity and a norm to access housing, health care and education (see, for example, Graeber 2011; Lazzarato 2011, 2015; Soederberg 2014). Such analyses are less directly concerned with, and hence less restricted by, the specific conceptual parameters of social stratification debates, and more interested in capturing the broad impact of economic shifts on social inequality. These perspectives argue that the need for a growing part of the population to access credit increases the power of creditors and that the asymmetrical creditor–debtor relation has become a constitutive and generalized social relation, one that is lived and structured as a class relation. This class relation is understood to be evident in how the necessity of debt directly benefits creditors, not least in extended opportunities to extract profits in the form of interest payments on loans, mortgages and other forms of contracted debt.

Although such analyses have a definite cultural valence, they nonetheless mistake what is an asset economy for a credit–debt economy. In their concern to emphasize that debt has become a requirement for everyday living, they tend to insufficiently recognize the central role of collateral: indebtedness is very often a necessary condition of asset holding. Most household debt, for example, is mortgage debt held by owner investors against residential property as a financial asset. The lack of attention to the asset dimension also means that these analyses have difficulty developing a systematic perspective on the dynamics of sustained and institutionally organized asset price inflation. The result is an overly neat and dichotomous model of class that is unable to conceptualize the stratifying effects of asset ownership.

Standing (2011) has edged closer to recognizing the role of assets in shaping class positions by pointing to a growing differentiation between a precariat class who live off casual and short-term labour contracts and a rentier class who live off the income flows from financial assets. But Standing's taxonomy of class remains too dichotomous and fails to account for the fact that significant proportions of the population have been included in the asset economy and that important class differences exist *within* the population of asset holders. In other words, to the extent that existing class models have been challenged, it takes the form of the supplementation of such models with an emphasis on the growth of rentier wealth concentrated in the very top echelons of society (see Atkinson et al. 2017).

Even in more recent work, where Standing (2016) has added more complexity to his analysis of class, this supplementation continues to be present. Here, Standing remains committed to the idea that it is only the very top layers of the class structure – comprising of what he describes as a plutocracy, an elite, the salariat and proficians (freelance professionals) – that gain most of their income from capital and rent rather than from labour. These rentier groups, living mostly off income flows from financial assets, sit above three classes who gain 'nothing in rent' (Standing 2016: 28): a shrinking proletariat, an expanding precariat, and an abandoned and growing 'lumpen-precariat' who struggle to sustain life. While clearly wanting to add more nuance to his understanding of the shaping of class positions, nonetheless, within this, Standing persists with the idea that different kinds of rentier classes have been 'super-imposed on preceding class structures' (p. 27) and that the growth of rentier wealth is only at issue for the very top tiers of society. This is where his analysis, despite its more radical overtones, displays structural similarities with Piketty's analysis.

As discussed, Piketty's findings on wealth-based inequalities have led to a preoccupation with the emergence of the super-rich, especially with the increasing wealth gap between the richest 1% and remaining 99% of populations and with the lifeworlds of the very wealthy (see, for example, Baldwin et al. 2019; Dorling 2014; Forrest et al. 2017; Glucksberg & Burrows 2016; Harrington 2016; Sherman 2017). Among sociologists this has led to calls for a new focus on the super-rich, especially on how this group might be crystallizing as a social and cultural class (see, for example, Atkinson et al. 2017; Burrows & Knowles, 2019; Burrows et al. 2017; Cunningham & Savage 2017; Savage 2014). As Savage (2014: 603) has put it, '[the] fundamental point which Piketty's class analysis leads to ... is the need to focus on the very wealthy, and how far this group might indeed be crystallizing as a class'. While it is certainly the case that there is a greater concentration of capital gains among the top percentiles of the wealth and income distribution, a focus only on the very wealthy fails to grasp how large proportions of the population are included in the asset economy, how asset inflation is a long-term political project and how class differences exist within the population of asset holders. In other words, an exclusive focus on the super-wealthy obscures just how profound the effects of the asset economy have been in reshaping the social structure, and it leaves intact (implicitly or explicitly) a more basic and structural model of class as based on work and employment.

Class and generation

To capture this reshaping, we might propose a class scheme that is analogous to Marxist and Weberian schemes but that identifies asset ownership as the key distributor and driver of life chances. In figure 1 we offer such a scheme. It has been developed with specific reference to the Australian context and it reflects some of the institutional specificities of that context (which are elaborated in detail in Adkins et al. 2019). But given the shared pathways across Anglo-capitalist societies, it has relevance well beyond the specifics of the Australian case and hence can also be considered an ideal type. It differentiates five classes defined by their relationships to asset ownership, and especially to property ownership: from investors who live off the income generated from diversified portfolios of assets through to non-asset owning classes (renters and the homeless). The scheme therefore captures the stratifying effects of asset ownership and property inflation. While the scheme is classificatory (outlining how different relationships to asset ownership define class positions), it also recognizes that these classes exist in relation to one another: positions in the asset-based class scheme concern the abilities of classes relative to each other to own assets and to benefit from asset holdings. Renters who are dependent on income from labour, for example, are likely to be servicing the mortgages of landlord investors and hence providing the conditions of possibility for investors to enhance

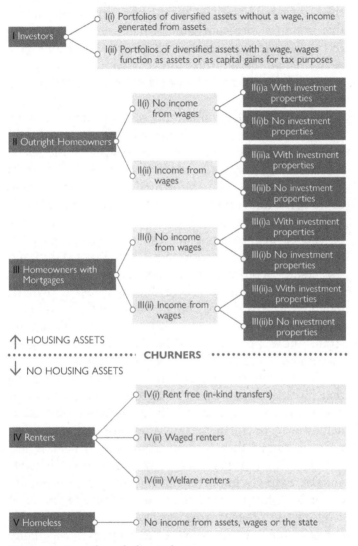

Figure 1. Asset-based class scheme
Source: Adkins et al. 2019: 18.

their asset holdings and asset-based capital gains. But this is not a zero-sum game where benefits for some rest on losses for others: asset-based class positions have been constituted and distributed institutionally via the macro-level twin processes of asset price inflation and wage moderation.

In foregrounding different relationships to asset ownership, our scheme makes explicit the full implications of the asset economy for reshaping the social structure. The scheme therefore moves away from simplistic models of a bifurcated class structure (e.g. of rentiers and renters or of creditors and debtors) and articulates a top, bottom, and a middle range of classes defined by complex relationships to asset ownership (including mortgaged home ownership and ownership of investment properties). It captures how the population as a whole (outright asset owners, indebted asset owners and non-asset owners alike) is incorporated into the economy of assets and demonstrates how positions within the hierarchy of asset ownership overdetermine the wage relationship.

It is important here to reiterate that we are not claiming that income from wages has become unimportant – it manifestly has not, and indeed for those without assets it may well be an increasingly precarious lifeline. The point is rather that income from employment is less and less itself a gateway to a middle-class lifestyle and increasingly important primarily as a determinant of one's ability to participate in the logic of the asset economy. In other words, our asset-based class scheme depicts a logic within which other sources of inequality are increasingly playing out. That also means that it is not a matter of simply tracing the 'interaction' between different forms of inequality. This is not necessarily a 'wrong' way of putting the matter, but it is nevertheless a misleading one: our claim is that other sources of inequality are increasingly absorbed into and refracted through the logic of the asset economy.

We should situate the generational dimension along similar lines. Even though we have argued that the generational dimension has come to play an increasingly important role in the construction of class, this dimension is not visible in the schema. This is because the role that the generational dimension plays is not an independent one – its growing prominence is a function of the rise of the asset economy. It is important here to differentiate our position from the way this issue is often presented in public debate. In recent years, an outpouring of academic, policy and popular publications has argued that the lock-out from asset ownership is taking place along generational lines (see, for example, Resolution Foundation 2018; Shaw 2018; Sternberg 2019; Willetts 2010; Wood & Griffiths 2019). According to this story, in the context of continued rises in house prices, stagnant wages and contingent modes of employment, the millennial generation (those born from 1981 to 2000) has been priced out from the key source of asset-based wealth – home ownership – and hence from the benefits of asset appreciation. The millennial predicament is then contrasted to the fortunes of the baby boomer generation (those born from 1946 to 1964) who, having enjoyed stable income flow from labour and much lower house prices, are seen as having been the prime beneficiaries of asset price appreciation (see, for example, Exley 2019; Gardiner 2016; Reeves 2018; Willetts 2010).

The generational perspective is certainly not an implausible way of framing the matter. In Australia, for example, since the early 2000s older households (age 55–65 and especially 65 plus) have captured most of the growth in household wealth, while the wealth of younger households (age 25–34) has been on the decline

(Daley & Wood 2014). In the UK, elderly households now hold more wealth than households of the same age a decade ago (Hood & Joyce 2017), and for 'the first time in British history, pensioner incomes after housing costs have caught up with those of working-age families' (Willetts 2019: 1). Millennials are earning less than their immediate Generation X (those born between 1965 and 1980) predecessors at the same stage of the life course, and this shift has taken place in an institutional context where defined benefit pension provision has been actively phased out, social housing stocks have been drastically reduced, and investments in human capital (and especially in education) are not yielding the returns they once did. Even when occupying the kinds of jobs that would have previously guaranteed access to home ownership, in the context of ever-rising house prices and stagnant wages, millennials typically find themselves unable to leverage their wages to access sufficient mortgage credit to enter the housing market. With the costs of private renting also rising, many find themselves also priced out of the rental market, especially in large urban centres (see, for example, Parkinson et al. 2019). As a consequence, the share of younger adults living with their parents is increasing (Clapham et al. 2014; Flynn & Schwartz 2017).

At face value, all this lends considerable support to the idea that the asset economy has given rise to a division operating along generational lines. The generational interpretation also resonates with attempts, emanating from cultural studies and literary scholarship, to capture the distinctive zeitgeist of the twenty-first century. Such cultural diagnoses have announced the end or 'cancellation of the future' (Fisher 2014), arguing that the contemporary capitalist imaginary is no longer driven by a viable sense of a better future that can be hopefully anticipated. Such assessments speak to the idea that the future of the current generation has been stolen by previous generations and that a generational contract has been broken. This connection becomes particularly relevant and powerful in discussions of student debt (especially in the US context), which have tended to stress that the modern form of indenture created by student loan debt in combination with the precarization of employment makes a mockery of the neoliberal idea of human capital. From this perspective, millennials therefore not only struggle to find an entry point into asset building, but lead lives that are shackled to the sunk investments and unforgivable debts of the past (Watlington 2019). With reference to the US case, Sternberg (2019: 75) has referred to the phenomenon of non-returning investments in education as 'human capital punishment'.

All this also makes comprehensible how generational analysis, long a discredited branch of sociology, is making a return to respectable social science. However, to the extent that such work has been successful, it is precisely because it has not severed the connections between generation and other social categories, much in the way that early twentieth-century sociologists such as Mannheim (1952 [1923]) understood the role of generation (e.g. Cooper 2017; McClanahan 2019; Woodman & Wyn 2015). Indeed, baby boomer scapegoating plays the powerful ideological function of diverting attention from issues of class, and the concern that we are stealing from future generations has become one the most significant rationales behind austerity policies. What a literal generational interpretation misses is precisely the logic of *inter*-generational dynamics. What distinguishes successive generations today is less a difference in absolute wealth holdings (after all, if asset price inflation continues its current trajectory, millennials will hold *more* absolute wealth than baby boomers) than a difference in *modes of access* to wealth: while older baby boomer generations were in a better position to buy property through wages alone, this option has become less accessible to younger generations who are increasingly dependent on the ability and willingness of their parents to lend or give them money for a deposit in order to enter the housing market (Adkins et al. 2019). The millennial phenomenon is so important not because that generation will be characterized by a natural solidarity vis-a-vis other generations, but precisely because it is in this generation that the fault-lines engendered by the asset economy are becoming most clearly visible.

The generational question is therefore best seen as part of a broader problem that revolves around the temporal structuration of the asset economy and the way in which the asset-driven production of class expresses itself through changing lifetimes. Fuelled by the work of C Wright Mills (1959) on the intersection of history and biography, sociologists and other social scientists have often turned to the concept of the life course when analysing how socio-economic context influences how people's lives are ordered and lived. This idea of a specific life course has assumed new and heightened significance in the context of the transition to the asset economy. As central as the idea of a particular Keynesian life course was to the kinds of class analysis that we have discussed above, they also naturalized a particular life course featuring life events such as education, employment, saving and property ownership, family and reproduction, and retirement. Central to this understanding was the historically contingent assumption that wage-labour was not just a means of survival but a ticket to full socio-economic citizenship and middle-class status, as well as a way to transmit such middle-class status to the next generation.

Asset-driven lifetimes

The asset economy is ushering in a new political economy of life ordered by a distinctive temporal logic, one that we have referred to as the shift from a Keynesian to a Minskyan household. People are increasingly living, managing and planning asset-driven lives ordered by the speculative logics of asset appreciation. To survive in the asset economy, and especially to hold on to assets that may generate long-run returns, requires the active management of one's balance sheet. Assets are not static forms of property with stable and predictable values but are exposed to often volatile market valuations. Moreover, assets are typically financed through debt that requires constant servicing, necessitating the continuous management of income streams (including income from labour) to generate enough cash liquidity to meet those commitments. The temporal delays that exist between asset building, asset appreciation, and the generation of future income streams are highly consequential. Funding and holding an asset is a speculative affair, and liquidity is therefore the lifeblood of the Minskyan household in a way that it was not for the Keynesian household (Adkins 2019; Konings 2018). Liquidity is like oxygen, and even a temporary shortage of it can have far-reaching consequences, making the difference between speculative buoyancy or deathlike stagnation.

The notion of the life course suggests an ordered sequence of irreversible life stages that was attuned to the organization of life in the post-war era. But the suspensions, delays, deferrals and discontinuities characteristic of asset-based lives mean that they are often not lived as a sequence of chronologically ordered events. This is nowhere more evident than in the ways that major life events, from finishing education through paying off mortgages to leaving paid employment, are being delayed across the board and often never finished. Many young adults are, for example, experiencing deferred independence due to the seeming intractability of making one's own life in the asset economy, and especially making the leap of moving out of the parental home in the face of rising housing and rent prices as well as precarious wages. In Australia, as in the US and the UK, the age at which people are making their first home purchase is rising. Between 1981 and 2016 the typical age at which a first home was purchased increased by nine years from age 24 to age 33 (Chomik 2019). There has been an accompanying increase in the age at which young adults exit the parental home. From 2007 to 2011 the share of young adults (age 18–34) living in the parental home rose by 11% in the UK and in the US by 4% to reach an all-time high of 36% (Flynn & Schwarzt 2017). Some may use the opportunities afforded by extended dwelling in the parental home to save for a down payment on a first home, but even those who leave may return in the context of liquidity stress. Indeed, the 'boomerang effect' is a fully-fledged feature of life in the asset economy (Arundel & Lennartz 2017).

These kinds of deferrals and non-linear movements are certainly not limited to the lives of younger adults: they are just as likely to be experienced by older cohorts. In the post-war era mortgage payments and non-mortgaged home ownership were timed to end close to the end of working lives so that retirement could be lived free of mortgage debt. But in present-day Anglo-capitalist societies there are significant increases in the numbers of retirees with mortgage debt (Ong & Wood 2019). In such circumstances, working lives may be indefinitely extended well beyond the retirement ages associated with the post-war era to ensure that liabilities can be met and that lives remain liquid. But the demands of liquidity nonetheless mean that retirement from work may be in a constant state of deferral. Alternatively, older households may draw down on other assets such as superannuation to maintain household liquidity. Even retired householders who own their homes outright are remortgaging by using their homes as collateral to release equity to ensure liquidity to fund life in the here and now. Such equity releases are increasingly prevalent among retirees in Anglo-capitalist societies and have been made possible by a range of innovative consumer finance products, including lifetime and reverse mortgages (Bridge et al. 2010; Butrica & Mudrazija 2016; Fox O'Mahony & Overton 2015; Ong et al. 2014).

For older households, the fight for buoyancy may therefore have multiple dimensions. 'Downsizing' to unlock the market value of the home is perhaps the most well-known strategy. But this is only really an effective option for those who have homes in urban centres where there have been significant housing price increases. Another is to sell up and move into the homes of adult children (Liu et al. 2015). Such moves enable the creation of a consolidated intergenerational household balance sheet. But for many people, especially those in the early to mid-stages of asset building, and even when the market value of homes outstrips mortgage debt, options to consolidate may simply be unavailable. Here, the stark reality is defined by the need to stay afloat in the context of mortgage debt payments, stagnant wages and depreciating human capital. Attempts to offset human capital depreciation may include further investment in human capital as well as multiple jobs.

One way of understanding what is at stake in asset-based lives and the distinctive temporal logic organizing them – which resonates with how our class scheme uses the 'churners' to distinguish between those who are able to participate in inflationary asset dynamics and those who aren't – might be to say that the asset economy structures class through a separation of those who are able to participate in the upwards dynamics of speculative asset valuation from those who are unable to graduate from the short temporal horizons of the commodity economy to the longer speculative horizons of the asset economy. Along such lines, Tadiar (2012, 2013) has advanced a distinction between those with lives that can be capitalized to yield future returns and those whose lives are merely commodified, unable to store or retain value and therefore easily disposable. Tadiar therefore views lifetimes in present-day capitalism as divided between the expansive, future-oriented time of speculation and the decaying, diminishing time of the commodity.

That also explains why even more or less conscious attempts to stay out of the asset economy and to live a simpler, 'merely commodified' life are fraught with difficulties. Renting on a particular income will seem viable for some time, but the upward pressure on house prices eventually also pushes up rents. Refusing to save money and invest in the stock market is no longer possible now that even in the most generous welfare states public provision has dwindled to levels that make supplementary private income a real necessity. Indeed, even just getting a decent job that would (at least for some time) permit a commodity-based existence now almost everywhere requires investment in human capital – that is, borrowing funds to finance tertiary education and training. Neoliberalism made real the idea that when you sell your labour, you are not simply involved in a monetary transaction but are able to earn income on your human capital. By this logic, education is an investment in one's own future self, meant to build skills that will generate returns and achieve capital gains and so allow for the repayment of the debt incurred to build them (Brown 2015). But of course, wage stagnation means that the asset of human capital has been subject to devaluation, even if the debt assumed to build it remains fully intact. This creates a version of the 'underwater mortgage' phenomenon – the need to maintain payments on an (undischargeable) debt that is larger than the asset it purchased. In other words, what the idea of a bifurcation between an asset economy and a commodity economy fails to capture is how all of us are now exposed to the logics of asset appreciation and depreciation, inflation and deflation.

Nowhere have the effects of this dual logic become more visible than in the realities of a debt-financed liberal arts education, especially in the US (but very similar tensions are beginning to show up in other countries). Young graduates are increasingly locked into debt servicing, living a life that is constantly drained of liquidity, deprived of possibilities for making new investments and changing course. And this also means that the road to home ownership becomes that much harder. For people who are currently entering adulthood, the bar for attaining a middle-class existence is simply higher than it was for previous generations.

As already indicated, this sense of permanent, inescapable crisis is prominent in diagnoses of the zeitgeist. A common lament here is that a sense of future has been lost: that there is an absence of a progressive forward movement in and through time. Hence we hear about the 'slow cancellation of the future' (Fisher 2014: 8), the 'abortion of the future' (Krause-Franzten 2019: 2), life 'after the future' (Berardi 2011: 163), and 'the strange sensation of living ... without time' (Lazzarato 2011: 47). The idea here is that life becomes a series of moments of bare survival, forced participation in a game of which the outcome has been pre-empted by the existence of a debt to the past that can never be discharged. Lisa Baraitser (2017) talks of a new kind of temporal experience, where time doesn't really flow as it used to, which she calls 'enduring time'. Similar concepts are Eric Cazdyn's (2012) notion of 'the new chronic', where we're always licking our wounds without hope for a full recovery; or Lauren Berlant's (2011) idea of 'slow death'. We have already flagged our reservations about the idea of the end of the future. It seems that no matter how disaffected we might be, we're still intensely concerned with what's coming and the possibility of a better future. At the same time, it is undeniably the case that these formulations are capturing something essential of the experience of having to design one's life while being dragged down by a massive amount of 'negative net worth'. It is therefore important to entertain the idea that we are witnessing something more paradoxical here.

We have seen that often successful performance in the asset-driven economy is contingent on the possibility of accessing liquidity, of buying time. This becomes visible most spectacularly in situations of full-blown bailouts: when the market as a whole is being rocked by waves of instability, the largest institutions can often just stay still and ride out the turmoil, counting on liquidity assistance and bailouts. But ways for key financial actors to defer payment pressures have been embedded in the most basic mechanisms of financial governance. And this of course is at odds with a more familiar image of capital (and in particular finance), where we associate it with speed and acceleration (e.g. Rosa 2013). And we can see something similarly paradoxical at work on the other end of the distributional scale. Far from any sense of prospect or futurity disappearing, contemporary capitalism induces an anomaly that is best described as 'frenetic inactivity' or 'non-stop inertia' (Southwood 2011). Something must be done because our sense of the future is all too real; it's just that often there isn't anything particularly effective to be done. We must be entrepreneurial and actively choose from a menu featuring only bad options, each of which will further stunt our growth and flourishing (Elliott 2018). What we end up with is an exhausting, nerve-racking combination of need for constant vigilance in combination with the absence of clear rewards. Elliott has called this 'suffering agency', a paradoxical state that demands constant alertness and preparedness but is simultaneously experienced for all intents and purposes as pre-decided.

Again, this affective register should not be taken as a uniform transition to a new form of alienation experienced by a particular generation. The idea that entire generational cohorts have been locked out from asset ownership and have been dispossessed by older generations becomes instantly problematic once issues of inheritance and intergenerational wealth transfers are brought into the picture. Many structural impossibilities (graduating without debt; saving for a down payment; being able to do the two years of unpaid internships that interesting, well-paid professions increasingly require) become entirely viable if one has the good fortune to have wealthy parents who can provide 'bailouts'.

In the context of sustained increases in house prices and the participation of substantial parts of populations in Anglo-capitalist countries in (potential or actual) capital gains through home ownership, an increased proportion of older households now stand ready to transfer wealth to their adult children through the mechanism of inheritance. Indeed, younger generations are now much more likely to expect to receive an inheritance than their predecessors (Daley & Wood 2014; Hood & Joyce 2017). There has also been a sharp increase in inter vivos intergenerational transfers of wealth for the purpose of purchasing a home in Anglo-capitalist countries (Christophers 2018; Flynn & Schwartz 2017; Köppe 2018; Ronald & Lennartz 2018), with young adults increasingly relying on the ability and willingness of their parents to lend or give them money for a down payment in order to enter the housing market. Inheritance has historically served as a critical mechanism for the transfer of private wealth from one generation to the next, and has done so especially for the very wealthiest (see, for example, Beckert 2008). In the asset economy, however, where asset holding is a key determinant of life chances and has spread well beyond the 1%, inheritance and inter vivos transfers take on a new significance.

First, these wealth transfers are becoming key mechanisms for across-the-board social stratification: no longer merely a way for the very wealthiest to pass on their wealth to their children, they are becoming an important variable in the reproduction of wealth-based inequalities and asset-based class positions across the socio-economic spectrum. Receiving a cash transfer from parents for a deposit on a property or having parents who are willing to put up their own property as security on the purchase of another property can be decisive for the ability of young adults to enter the property market. In the Australian case, young adults who are competing against each other and investors to make a first home purchase are significantly more likely to purchase a home if they receive financial help from their parents (Barrett et al. 2015a, 2015b; Simon & Stone 2017). Indeed, the sum total of these commitments has been estimated to make the Australian 'Bank of Mum and Dad' akin to a mid-size home lender (Kohler 2018). There is also growing evidence that parents are not just engaging in direct transfers of wealth but that they are also taking on debt, guaranteeing loans and releasing equity to help their children onto the property ladder (Udagawa & Sanderson 2017; Yeates 2016).

In the UK we can see similar trends, with increasing numbers of younger people receiving support from older generations to make a first home purchase. It has been estimated that parents are involved in more than 25% of all first-time home purchases (Ronald & Lennartz 2018) and that up to 60% of first-time buyers expect to need financial assistance from family members (House of Lords Select Committee 2019). The effects of these transfers have been found to be similar to those for the Australian case in that they significantly strengthen young people's ability to purchase a dwelling. In addition, the use of intergenerational financial products that enable parents to assist their adult children to make first home purchases, including intergenerational mortgages, as well as loans, equity release and remortgaging, is on the rise (House of Lords Select Committee 2019).

Second, in the context of sustained asset appreciation, inheritances, and especially residential property bequests, come to have a distinctive speculative dimension. Inheritance is no longer a passive transfer of property that occurs by default following someone's death. Instead, inheritance becomes a series of strategic decisions regarding how to position one's children in the asset economy. Inter vivos wealth transfers are essentially forms of advanced inheritance that need to be put to work in the asset economy – leveraged to serve as the basis of asset ownership. Beneficiaries receive not just a one-off lump sum but an opening into the wealth effects of asset ownership.

The growth of such intergenerational wealth transfers means that, rather than simply being in a state of decomposition, a generational contract is in operation in the asset economy. This contract no longer functions through the redistributive transfer mechanisms of the state; it operates through a re-galvanized, re-invented and re-formed family (Cooper 2017; Flynn 2017; Ronald & Lennartz 2018; Ronald et al. 2017). In the context of the retrenchment of the social state, the stagnation of wages, runaway housing prices and increases in household wealth, in Anglo-capitalist countries the family therefore now operates as a key source of economic security.

Flynn and Schwartz (2017: 476) have argued that these changes mean that Anglo-capitalist countries are moving away from a market-based model and are becoming more Southern European in character. But this is to understate the degree to which the re-familialization trend is integrated into – rather than being a departure from – the logic of financialized capitalism. The effects of the asset economy cannot be grasped by assuming that Anglo-capitalist societies are starting to resemble other kinds or types in a socio-structural sense, or that the asset economy has returned us to a world that existed before the innovations of the twentieth-century welfare state. The asset economy is characterized by its own distinctive logics, which have transformed the social structure in specific ways. In this chapter we have stressed that these transformations have involved a far-going restructuring of the class structure, a resetting of the dynamics of the household and a reorganization of the political economy of life. Class positions have become asset-based, the Minskyan household has replaced the Fordist household, and these trends have led to the emergence of asset-driven lifetimes, shaped profoundly by the dynamics of appreciation and depreciation and the struggle for liquidity.

Conclusion

It is increasingly common for mainstream organizations to ring the alarm bell about the social and political consequences of growing social inequalities. The OECD is worried about the decline of the middle class, *The Economist* fears the rise of millennial socialism, and many of the admonitions that the *Financial Times* issues to its financial establishment readership would not look out of place in a much more politically progressive publication. This book has argued that the role of assets is central to the social transformations that provoke such concerns. Several decades of asset inflation have produced a new logic of inequality, and asset ownership is becoming more important than employment as a determinant of class position. We have characterized this in terms of the transition from the Keynesian to the Minskyan household, which has uprooted the function of (male breadwinner) employment and the specific notion of a life course associated with it to create more fluid and unpredictable lifetimes and to press them more fully into the service of asset building and the speculative valuation of assets.

This recognition of the structuring role of assets is important in order to be able to move beyond the acknowledgement of across-the-board increases in multiple dimensions of inequality (e.g. Dorling 2018; Milanovic 2018; Stilwell 2019) and to be able to pinpoint more precisely the source of contemporary social problems. For instance, the kind of mainstream organizations we just cited tend to be concerned less about inequality and more with its manifestations and potential political fallout. This typically means a focus on the implications of growing inequality for perceived social mobility and equality of opportunity. The OECD (2018) has stressed how those at the bottom ends of income ranges have become more immobile while those at the top of income distributions are hoarding their privileges and have become more effective in passing on their advantages to their children. A double dynamic of stalling and hoarding means that 'people at the bottom are less likely to move up, and ... people at the top are even less likely to slide down' (OECD 2018: 32). This marks an important shift away from the early post-war period when upward social mobility was a practical (if always limited) reality made possible by changes to the occupational structure, especially the expansion of managerial and professional occupations (Bukodi & Goldthorpe 2018; Elliot & Machin 2018; Friedman & Laurison 2019). However, in describing the stalling of mobility as a 'broken social elevator' (OECD 2018: 3), the OECD implies that mobility can be fixed by returning to the social structures characteristic of the post-war era. In this way, it continues to model social mobility in terms of the movement across employment-based income scales. And it is the relevance of such an employment-focused model that we have questioned in this book. Even if we do not question the limitations of a focus on mobility alone, the tendency to analyse that problem through a work-centred understanding of inequality compromises our ability to understand it and to formulate effective policies to address it.

In explaining the logic of the asset economy, we have drawn on work in heterodox political economy, in particular the ideas of Minsky. But we have shifted the emphasis away from where discussions of Minsky normally place it, which is on the unsustainable nature of systematic overindebtedness. Our main conceptual point here has been that there exists no objective tipping point, an amount of debt beyond which structures of debt become unsustainable, and that this is ultimately a social and institutional question. Minsky moved away from the idea that assets had a true or real underlying value that was to prevail in the long run. In that sense, Minsky was what we might refer to as a post-foundational thinker who contested the idea that the quality of our socio-economic constructions can be understood by assessing it against an external or theoretically derived standard. As long as one relies on the idea that assets have specific underlying values, it is easy to shift and start talking about the problem of debt in an abstract way – as if there is something inherently contradictory about the intensified engagement of the future that debt represents. In this book we have emphasized that we should not reduce the economy of assets to an economy of debt. That tendency inadvertently imports too many of the framing concepts of orthodox understandings of the market into our critique of neoliberalism. The analysis of the asset economy needs to be framed not by the inevitably moralistic Polanyian concern with market disembedding, but through a focus on the speculative valuation and debt-driven financing of assets.

If we have kept our distance from structuralist economic analyses, we have also tried to steer clear of more journalistic and event-focused accounts. There is currently a growing recognition that house prices in large cities have become unaffordable, that they play havoc with the ability of young people to achieve key life events at the same time as their parents, and that policies like quantitative easing are making this problem significantly worse. But the way these phenomena are described often reflects a wish to reduce the problem to discrete policies or specific political alliances – as if the mere election of a new set of political elites could significantly change this configuration, or as if the problem here neatly aligns with political party platforms.

As is so often the case, there exists a certain complementarity between the concern with deep structures and the tendency to overprivilege political choice and agency. Such approaches sustain each other insofar as one highlights elements that are not readily visible in the other. What is missing is a mid-range understanding of how the asset economy has changed the social logic of stratification and inequality, of how the double dynamic of human capital depreciation and asset appreciation has produced a new kind of society, characterized by a distinctive class structure.

In that sense, our intervention in this book can be read as examining the conceptual parameters of current neoliberalism debates, where questions about the relative importance of structural economic imperatives on the one hand and political and ideological struggles on the other have been central. Recent contributions have emphasized that both of these dimensions matter, and increasingly the dominant tendency is to portray neoliberalism as a project of relentless commodification that survives because of the strategies deployed by political elites and how these obscure the ways neoliberalism harms the interests and preferences of the bulk of the population (Dardot & Laval 2019; Duménil & Lévy 2013; Mirowski 2013). Such analytical recombinations of the categories of state and market make it hard to see what is new about the present era, or to understand how neoliberalism was ever viable without resorting to fairly crude notions of ideology.

Of course, people making money from assets instead of labour is not by itself a new phenomenon. From that angle, it might seem that neoliberalism does in fact merely mean the resurrection of the rentier. But this would be to ignore the extent to which making money from assets has become democratized (and also the extent to which asset ownership itself is 'work', in the sense that it often lacks the glamour and leisure that we associate with rentierism). Of central importance here is the fact that the policies that have enabled returns on assets to outstrip those on labour took place in a historical and institutional setting where property ownership had already to a significant extent become democratized. This is where our story differs from that offered by Piketty, who sees asset appreciation in terms of a return to the plutocracy of the gilded age. While we are by no means concerned to deny the reality of the 1%, the reason why we are talking of an 'economy of assets' is that the 1% phenomenon should be seen as part of a wider logic of asset ownership that includes a larger percentage of households. Putting a spotlight on the growing wealth of the very top is a perfectly legitimate political strategy with significant mobilizational capacity, but such an orientation is not by itself capable of explaining why the trends that it identifies are so resilient and embedded. Neoliberalism may be approaching its own limits and contradictions, but these cannot be understood through the Polanyian lens of reversals: just as post-war Keynesianism effected lasting changes, so neoliberalism built something that needs to be understood on its own terms.

The future of the asset economy is a social question, to do with how societies have become structured and how these patterns express themselves in different contexts. For instance, as we have argued, quantitative easing may certainly be a problematic policy in the sense that it benefits asset holders over those who hold no assets, and wealthy asset holders over middle-class asset holders, but this is not entirely a contingent outcome: given the structures that have been built up over the course of the neoliberal era, central banks have few options other than to feed liquidity into financial markets. To understand how this kind of policy lock-in occurs – how societies and their governments end up in positions where they have no choice but to pursue policies that they experience as increasingly problematic – we have pushed our political economy analysis into a more sociological direction to shed light on the different constituencies underpinning these policies.

Our analytical focus on assets as an alternative to the more common focus on commodification is not meant to deny that many things that used to be provided through public institutions are now organized through price mechanisms, and this has everything to do with deregulation and public austerity. But it is not clear that we can understand the growth of inequality through this lens alone – increasingly, the charge of commodification is primarily a cultural criticism, remaining within the parameters of the orthodox image of the market while giving it a negative normative twist. Marx foregrounded the commodity in order to analyse a specific kind of exploitation, a specific source of inequality, and a specific kind of society: one based in the exploitation of wage-labour. Such exploitation is of course far from absent in the contemporary world, but it has been the argument of this book that we can no longer view it as the driving force of inequality.

One way of capturing this is that the logic of inequality production has assumed a more 'topological' quality (Lury 2013; Lury et al. 2012): it works less and less through extraction and appropriation, and increasingly through the inflation and deflation of temporally situated claims. The speculative logic of the asset economy implies a specific politics of valuation and measurement as performative, as processes that do not passively represent a pre-given objective value but actively format the socio-economic terrain and its practices. This idea has received considerable attention at a theoretical level, for instance, in value-form theory (Elson 1979), the autonomist rejection of labour as the measure of value (Negri 1999), and in the pragmatist critique which understands value not as an ontological given but as practice (Muniesa 2011). But the implications of such post-foundationalist or anti-essentialist understandings of value have often been left hanging when it comes to macro-level questions of political economy.

Minsky is helpful here too – in particular his two-price model (2008 [1986]), which distinguishes the process that governs asset prices from the logic that determines consumer prices. The former involves elements of time, speculation and uncertainty that are absent from the latter. It is from this angle that we can understand that the official focus on consumer price inflation as measured through the consumer price index (CPI), and the resulting common perception that we live in an inflation-less world, brackets the inflationary logic and distributional effects of the asset economy in a highly consequential way. The CPI is based on a rigorous distinction between consumption and investment.

Anything that can be thought of as an investment – an outlay of funds that is meant to generate returns in the future – is therefore not included. In a particular historical context, this made considerable sense: the CPI was meant to serve as an index that would be able to keep track of changes in the cost of living for the purpose of calibrating expectations around wage growth (and assuaging working-class suspicions that the value of their wages was being eroded by rising average prices). But even though we have come to think of it as such, the CPI is not a natural, objective indicator of the general level of prices. There exists no neutral way to measure a general price level – everything depends on the purpose for which an index is constructed and how it is calculated (Hayes 2011). To think of our current world as one where the value of money is stable and predictable ('neutral', in the language of orthodox economic theory) is to divert attention from the distributional effects of asset inflation. And when it comes to neatly separating consumption from investment, the assetized home represents a particular problem. The exclusion of property prices from official inflation indexes increasingly militates against our understanding of everyday life: getting annual wage increases to match inflation when house prices go up by 10% a year means effectively that one's standard of living is declining.

As we have seen, the promises of democratized asset ownership and universal wealth effects ran up against limits in almost all areas, and it has been in the area of housing that they found more lasting traction. The crisis of 2007–8 meant a significant challenge to this image of property ownership as a democratic generator of wealth. Defying widespread expectations, housing markets in large urban centres have rebounded with a vengeance since the crisis (Jordà et al. 2019). But the problematic effects of this are increasingly visible and are a growing source of concern for politicians and policymakers. Central here is the concentration of the benefits of property inflation among the already propertied and the exclusion of aspiring middle-class households from the housing market. The same (CPI-adjusted) salary that would have allowed someone to buy into the property market ten years ago no longer allows that, as in many places property prices have doubled in the meantime.

Any policies that may be designed to address this problem and to improve housing affordability inevitably are double-edged: measures that bring property ownership in reach for some (e.g. lower interest rates) simultaneously work to push prices up further and to put them out of reach for aspiring homeowners. In January 2020 the Australian Federal Government introduced a new initiative – the First Home Loan Deposit Scheme – designed to support first-time buyers on low and middle incomes by waiving the fees and insurance costs usually associated with small deposit purchases. This scheme is certainly not the first of its kind in Australia and is one among many that have been implemented in Anglo-capitalist societies with the aim of assisting first-time buyers to get a foothold on the housing ladder. While such policies might be understood to be successful on their own terms, they do nothing to address the systemic problem of rising property prices (see, for example, Daley & Coates 2018).

In the face of this apparent inability of governments to put in place meaningful policy initiatives to redress the affordability problem, progressives have certainly not neglected to advance more radical proposals (see, for example, Christophers 2019; Ryan Collins 2018; Stein 2019). But such approaches often fail to recognize that house price inflation is not a discrete problem, but a key pillar of the structuring of neoliberal societies that is deeply embedded in their operations. Central banks, for example, are acutely aware that raising interest rates in order to contain the growth of housing prices is no straightforward matter; their anticipation of the potential fallout increasingly means they refrain from using this policy instrument. Relatedly, when given the option of voting for more radical solutions to address the housing affordability problem and the growing wealth inequalities that accompany it, electorates have often voted against them. The Australian case is again paradigmatic: during the campaign for the 2019 Federal election, the Australian Labor Party proposed abolishing tax breaks targeted at property investors and reforming property-based capital gains tax discounts. The election – described as 'all about property' (Kehoe 2018) – returned a Liberal–National Party coalition with a neoliberal business-as-usual approach to property prices and property taxes. This outcome tells us much about the role of property ownership and property prices in the dynamics of neoliberal societies: significant parts of national electorates (enough to return political parties to office) are invested in ongoing asset inflation, tax concessions for property investors and minimal or zero inheritance tax. In this way, housing has become a significant generator of inequality.

The way in which politics and policymaking in the area of housing have become locked into a logic whereby they can only solve short-term problems by making the problem worse in the long run is reflective of deep contradictions at the heart of the asset economy. In mainstream debate, these contradictions have been registered in the rise of secular stagnation theory (Summers 2016). The basic idea here – that capitalism has entered a stage of long-term stagnation, where each recovery is turning out to be more lacklustre than the last one – is essentially a variation on Piketty's blunter r>g – which expresses the belief that, if left unchecked, capitalism will evolve into a rentiers' paradise. Each theory in its own way argues that present-day economies are characterized by too many accumulated financial claims in relation to the productive capacity of the real economy. It is certainly true that, with each round of quantitative easing, infusions of liquidity have more and more difficulty trickling down to lower levels. But the idea that capital has run out of steam remains a metaphysical claim.

Much like the notion that time has come to a standstill, the idea that the wheels of economic progress have stopped turning provides an interesting gloss on the zeitgeist, but it does not provide a compelling analytical frame. What Summers and Piketty try to capture in terms of natural economic laws is much better understood as a function of specific interests associated with particular constituencies and class positions. This is well illustrated by the example of housing policy: the difficulty consists in catering to the expectations of an existing constituency of middle-class homeowners without raising the barriers of entry for the rest of society. This policy conundrum is only comprehensible if we understand how a middle-class politics of asset democratization has ended up undermining the conditions of its own viability. There is, then, no necessary *economic* end to the logic of asset price appreciation – no final reckoning with fundamental value or the real economy. But if there is no logical or necessary economic transition before us, it seems clear that we are living through some kind of political shift that consists in the growing difficulty of convincing electorates that asset-based, credit-enabled aspiration will work.

This is most visible in the economic and political volatilities that are increasingly seen to characterize the millennial generation. Throughout this book, we have been highly critical of any attempt to separate the generational dimension from the class dimension, but we have also emphasized that the new logic of class and inequality cannot be understood without recognizing the generational dimension. It is in the millennial generation that the economic fault-lines produced by several decades of neoliberal policies are becoming visible, and where we find an increasingly intense dependence on family wealth as a determinant of whether one will flourish or languish in the asset economy. As we saw, *The Economist* is worrying that this may foster critical ideas about capitalism. We probably should be far more worried about the possibility that ongoing social polarization will feed into Trump-style fusions of populism and authoritarianism.

As we have argued, the institutional logic through which the asset economy has taken shape offers no easy ways out, no readily available policy options that can mitigate the problems that it has engendered. Unless those institutional parameters are reconfigured in fundamental ways, the asset economy will continue to polarize and trigger social responses that threaten existing mechanisms for the production of political legitimacy and social cohesion. Giving voice to this sense of accelerating economic polarization and concomitant political trends, Malcolm Harris (2017: 227–8) in his book *Kids These Days* says of his own generation that they will end up as 'fascists or revolutionaries, one or the other'. Of course, the need to make such political choices is not confined to members of that generation, and that only underscores what is at stake in the rapid polarization of political options. And that means that the socialist affinities that give *The Economist* and its establishment readership such anxiety may well be the only viable alternative to a future shaped by the opportunistic political manipulation of increasingly volatile public sentiment fostered by growing economic inequality.

References

Aalbers M & Christophers B (2014) 'Centering housing in political economy', *Housing, Theory and Society* 31(4): 373–94.

Adkins L (2018) *The Time of Money*. Stanford, CA: Stanford University Press.

Adkins L (2019) 'Social reproduction in the neoliberal era: payments, leverage and the Minskian household', *Polygraph* 27: 19–33.

Adkins L, Cooper M & Konings M (2019) 'Class in the 21st century: asset inflation and the new logic of inequality', *Environment and Planning A: Economy and Space*. DOI: 10.1177/0308518X19873673.

Arundel A & Lennartz C (2017) 'Returning to the parental home: boomerang moves of younger adults and the welfare regime context', *Journal of European Social Policy* 27(3): 276–94.

Atkinson A & Leigh A (2007) 'The distribution of top incomes in Australia'. In: Atkinson A & Piketty T (eds.) *Top Incomes Over the Twentieth Century*. Oxford: Oxford University Press.

Atkinson R, Parker S & Burrows R (2017) 'Elite formation, power and space in contemporary

London', *Theory, Culture and Society* 34(5–6): 179–200.

Baldwin S, Holroyd E & Burrows R (2019) 'Luxified troglodytism? Mapping the subterranean geographies of plutocratic London', *Architectural Research Quarterly* 23(3): 267–82.

Baraitser L (2017) *Enduring Time*. London: Bloomsbury.

Barrett G, Whelan S, Wood G & Cigdem M (2015a) 'How do intergenerational transfers affect housing and wealth?', *AHURI Research and Policy Bulletin* 203 (December). Melbourne, Vic: Australian Housing and Urban Research Institute Limited.

Barrett G, Cigdem M, Whelan S & Wood G (2015b) 'The relationship between intergenerational transfers, housing and economic outcomes', AHURI Final Report No. 250. Melbourne, Vic: Australian Housing and Urban Research Institute Limited.

Bartlett B (2013) 'The rise and fall of Carter's 1978 tax reform', *Tax Notes*, 18 February: 881–3.

Beckert J (2008) *Inherited Wealth*. Princeton, NJ: Princeton University Press.

Bell S (2004) *Australia's Money Mandarins: The Reserve Bank and the Politics of Money*. Cambridge: Cambridge University Press.

Bell S & Keating M (2018) *Fair Share: Competing Claims and Australia's Economic Future*. Melbourne, Vic: Melbourne University Press.

Bennett T, Emmison M & Frow J (1999) *Accounting for Taste: Australian Everyday Cultures*. Cambridge: Cambridge University Press.

Bennett T, Savage M, Silva EB, Warde A, Gayo-Cal M & Wright D (2009) *Culture, Class, Distinction*. Abingdon: Routledge.

Berardi F (2011) *After the Future*. Edinburgh: AK Press.

Berlant L (2011) *Cruel Optimism*. Durham, NC: Duke University Press.

Birch K (2017) 'Rethinking value in the bio-economy: finance, assetization, and the management of value', *Science, Technology and Human Values* 42(3): 460–90.

Block F & Somers MR (2014) *The Power of Market Fundamentalism: Karl Polanyi's Critique*. Cambridge, MA: Harvard University Press.

Blyth M (2013) *Austerity: The History of a Dangerous Idea*. Oxford: Oxford University Press.

Boltanski L & Chiapello E (2005) *The New Spirit of Capitalism*. London: Verso.

Bridge C, Adams T, Phibbs P, Mathews M & Kendig H (2010) 'Reverse mortgages and older people: growth factors and implications for retirement decisions', AHURI Final Report No. 146. Melbourne, Vic: Australian Housing and Urban Research Institute Limited.

Brink L & Teles SM (2017) *The Captured Economy: How the Powerful Enrich Themselves, Slow Down Growth, and Increase Inequality*. Oxford: Oxford University Press.

Brown W (2015) *Undoing the Demos: Neoliberalism's Stealth Revolution*. New York: Zone Books.

Bryan D & Rafferty M (2018) *Risking Together: How Finance is Dominating Everyday Life in Australia*. Sydney, NSW: University of Sydney Press.

Bukodi E & Goldthorpe J (2018) *Social Mobility and Education in Britain*. Cambridge: Cambridge University Press.

Burrows R & Knowles C (2019) 'The "haves" and the "have yachts": socio-spatial struggles in London between the "merely wealthy" and the "super-rich"', *Cultural Politics* 15(1): 72–87.

Burrows R, Webber R & Atkinson R (2017) 'Welcome to "Pikettyville"? Mapping London's alpha territories', *Sociological Review* 65(2): 184–201.

Butrica B & Mudrazija S (2016) *Home Equity Patterns Among Older American Households.* Washington, DC: Urban Institute.

Cahill D & Konings M (2017) *Neoliberalism.* Cambridge: Polity.

Canterbery ER (2000) *Wall Street Capitalism: The Theory of the Bondholding Class.* River Edge, NJ: World Scientific.

Cazdyn E (2012) *The Already Dead: The New Time of Politics, Culture and Illness.* Durham, NC: Duke University Press.

Cebul B (2019) 'Supply-side liberalism: fiscal crisis, post-industrial policy, and the rise of the new Democrats', *Modern American History* 2(2): 139–64.

Chomik R (2019) 'We're delaying major life events, and our retirement income system hasn't caught up', *The Conversation*, 25 November, www.theconversation.com/were-delaying-major-life-events-and-our-retirement-income-system-hasnt-caught-up-127231.

Christophers B (2018) 'Intergenerational inequality? Labour, capital, and housing through the ages', *Antipode* 50(1): 101–21.

Christophers B (2019) A tale of two inequalities: housing-wealth inequality and tenure inequality', *Environment and Planning A: Economy and Space.* DOI: 10.1177/0308518X19876946.

Chwieroth J & Walter A (2019) *The Wealth Effect: How the Great Expectations of the Middle Class Have Changed the Politics of Banking Crises.* Cambridge: Cambridge University Press.

Clapham D, MacKie P, Orford S, Thomas I & Buckley K (2014) 'The housing pathways of young people in the UK', *Environment and Planning A: Economy and Space* 46(8): 2016–31.

Connelly R, Gayle V & Lambert P (2016) 'A review

of occupation-based social classifications for social survey research', *Methodological Innovations* 9: 1–14.

Cooper M (2017) *Family Values: Between Neoliberalism and the New Social Conservatism.* New York: Zone Books.

Cooper M & Konings M (2015) 'Contingency and foundation: rethinking money, debt and finance after the crisis', *South Atlantic Quarterly* 114(2): 239–90.

Cribb J, Hood A & Hoyle J (2018) 'The decline of home ownership among young adults. Briefing note', Institute for Fiscal Studies, 16 February.

Crompton R (2008) *Class and Stratification.* Cambridge: Polity.

Cunningham N & Savage M (2017) 'An intensifying and elite city: new geographies of social class and inequality in contemporary London', *City* 21(1): 25–46.

Daley J & Coates B (2018) *Housing Affordability: Re-imagining the Australian Dream.* Melbourne, Vic: The Grattan Institute.

Daley J & Wood D (2014) *The Wealth of Generations.* Melbourne, Vic: The Grattan Institute.

Dardot P & Laval C (2019) *Never Ending Nightmare: The Neoliberal Assault on Democracy.* London: Verso.

Darling A (2007) HM Treasury press notice 134/07, Speech by the Chancellor of the Exchequer, the Rt Hon Alistair Darling MP, to the CBI Annual Conference, Business Design Centre, London, 27 November 2007.

Davidson P, Saunders P & Phillips J (2018) *Inequality in Australia 2018.* Sydney, NSW: ACOSS and UNSW Sydney.

Davis GF (2009) *Managed by the Markets: How Finance*

Re-shaped America. Oxford: Oxford University Press.

DeVore C (2015) 'Piketty Vs. Rognlie: Land use restrictions inflate housing values, drive wealth concentration', www.forbes.com/sites/chuckdevore/2015/07/22/piketty-vs-rognlie-land-use-restrictions-inflate-housing-values-drive-wealth-concentration.

Doganova L & Muniesa F (2015) 'Capitalization devices: business models and the renewal of markets'. In: Kornberger M, Jutesen L, Mouritsen J & Madsen AK (eds.) *Making Things Valuable.* Oxford: Oxford University Press.

Domitrovic B (2012) *Econoclasts: The Rebels Who Sparked the Supply-Side Revolution and Restored American Prosperity.* Wilmington, DE: Intercollegiate Studies Institute.

Dorling D (2014) *Inequality and the 1%.* London: Verso.

Dorling D (2018) *Peak Inequality: Britain's Ticking Time Bomb.* Bristol: Policy Press.

Duménil G & Lévy D (2005) 'Costs and benefits of neoliberalism: a class analysis'. In: Epstein GA (ed.) *Financialization and the World Economy.* Cheltenham: Edward Elgar.

Duménil G & Lévy D (2013) *The Crisis of Neoliberalism.* Cambridge, MA: Harvard University Press.

Elliot Major L & Machin S (2018) *Social Mobility and its Enemies.* London: Pelican.

Elliott J (2018) *The Micro-Economic Mode: Political Subjectivity and Contemporary Popular Aesthetics.* New York: Columbia University Press.

Elson D (1979) 'The value theory of labour'. In: Elson D (ed.) *Value: The Representation of Labour in Capitalism.* London: CSE Books.

Epstein GA & Jayadev A (2005) 'The rise of rentier incomes in OECD countries: financialization, central bank policy and labor solidarity'. In: Epstein GA (ed.) *Financialization and the World Economy.* Cheltenham: Edward Elgar.

Eslake S (2013) *Australian Housing Policy: 50 Years of Failure. Submission to the Senate Economics References Committee, 21st December.* Canberra, ACT: Parliament House Australia.

Exley D (2019) *The End of Aspiration: Social Mobility and Our Children's Fading Prospects.* Bristol: Policy Press.

Feher M (2009) 'Self-appreciation; or, the aspirations of human capital', *Public Culture* 21(1): 21–41.

Feher M (2018) *Rated Agency: Investee Politics in a Speculative Age.* New York: Zone Books.

Feldstein M (1978) 'Inflation and capital formation', *Wall Street Journal,* 27 July.

Feldstein M & Slemrod J (1978) 'Inflation and the excess taxation of capital gains on corporate stock', *National Tax Journal* 31(2): 107–18.

Financial Times (2019) 'Quantitative easing was the father of millennial socialism', 1 March.

Fisher M (2014) *Ghosts of My Life: Writings on Depression, Hauntology and Lost Futures.* Winchester: Zero Books.

Flynn L (2017) 'Delayed and depressed: from expensive housing to smaller families', *International Journal of Housing Policy* 17(3): 374–95.

Flynn LB & Schwartz HM (2017) 'No exit: social reproduction in an era of rising income inequality', *Politics and Society* 45(4): 471–503.

Forrest R, Koh SY & Wissink B (eds.) (2017) *Cities and the Super-Rich: Real Estate, Elite Practices and Urban Political Economies.* London: Springer.

Fox O'Mahony L & Overton L (2015) 'Asset-based welfare, equity release and the meaning of the owned home', *Housing Studies* 30(3): 392–412.

Fraser N & Jaeggi R (2018) *Capitalism: A Conversation in Critical Theory*. Cambridge: Polity.

Friedman S & Laurison D (2019) *The Class Ceiling: Why it Pays to be Privileged*. Bristol: Policy Press.

Fuller GW (2019) *The Political Economy of Housing Financialization*. Newcastle upon Tyne: Agenda.

Gane N (2015) 'Central banking, technocratic governance and the financial crisis: placing quantitative easing into question', *Sosiologia* 4: 381–96.

Gardiner L (2016) *Stagnation Generation: The Case for Renewing the Intergenerational Contract*. London: Resolution Foundation.

Glucksberg L & Burrows R (2016) 'Family offices and the contemporary infrastructures of dynastic wealth', *Sociologica, Italian Journal of Sociology Online* 2: 1–22. DOI: 10.2383/85289.

Goldthorpe J & Marshall G (1992) 'The promising future of class analysis: a response to recent critiques', *Sociology* 26(3): 381–400.

Goodhart C (2001) 'What weight should be given to asset prices in the measurement of inflation?', *The Economic Journal* 111(472): 335–56.

Graeber D (2011) *Debt: The First 5,000 Years*. New York: Melville House.

Graetz MJ (1976) 'The Democrats' tax program', *Wall Street Journal*, 11 August: 12.

Greenspan A (2002) *Issues for Monetary Policy, December 19*. Washington, DC: Federal Reserve Board.

Greider W (1989) *Secrets of the Temple: How the Federal Reserve Runs the Country*. New York: Simon and Schuster.

Guyer J (2015) 'Housing as "capital"', *Hau: Journal of Ethnographic Theory* 5(1): 495–500.

Hamnett C (1999) *Winners and Losers: Home Ownership in Modern Britain*. London: UCL Press.

Harrington B (2016) *Capital Without Borders: Wealth Managers and the One Percent.* Cambridge, MA: Harvard University Press.

Harris M (2017) *Kids These Days: Human Capital and the Making of Millennials.* New York: Little, Brown and Company.

Hayes M (2011) 'The social history of quantifying inflation: a sociological critique', *Journal of Economic Issues* 45(1): 97–112.

Head JG (1990) 'Australian tax reform: which way ahead?', *The Economic and Labour Relations Review* 1(2): 81–107.

Healey NM (1992) 'The Thatcher supply-side "miracle": myth or reality?', *The American Economist* 36(1): 7–12.

Henwood D (2003) *After the New Economy.* New York: The New Press.

Hibbs DA (1987) *The American Political Economy: Macroeconomics and Electoral Politics.* Cambridge, MA: Harvard University Press.

Hoerr JP (1988) *And the Wolf Finally Came: The Decline and Fall of the American Steel Industry.* Pittsburgh, PA: University of Pittsburgh Press.

Hood A & Joyce R (2017) *Inheritances and Inequality Across and Within Generations.* London: Institute for Fiscal Studies.

House of Lords Select Committee (2019) *Tackling Intergenerational Unfairness.* Select Committee on Intergenerational Fairness and Provision, Report of Session 2017–19, HL Paper 329. London: HMSO.

Hudson M (2012) *The Bubble and Beyond: Fictitious Capital, Debt Deflation and Global Crisis.* New York: ISLET.

Humphrys E (2019) *How Labour Built Neoliberalism: Australia's Accord, the Labour Movement and the Neoliberal Project.* Leiden: Brill.

Humphrys E & Cahill D (2017) 'How labour made neoliberalism', *Critical Sociology* 43(4–5): 669–84.

Jordà O, Knoll K, Kuvshinov D, Schularick M & Taylor AM (2019) 'The rate of return on everything, 1870–2015', *Quarterly Journal of Economics* 134(3): 1225–98.

Katic P & Leigh A (2016) 'Top wealth shares in Australia 1915–2012', *Review of Income and Wealth* 62(2): 209–22.

Kaufman BE (2004) *The Global Evolution of Industrial Relations: Events, Ideas and the IIRA*. Geneva: International Labour Office (ILO).

Keen S (2011) *Debunking Economics: The Naked Emperor Dethroned?* London and New York: Zed Books.

Keen S (2017) *Can We Avoid Another Financial Crisis?* Cambridge: Polity.

Kehoe J (2018) 'The next federal election will be about property. We explain the competing policies', *Financial Review*, 16 November, www.afr.com/property/the-next-federal-election-will-be-about-property-we-explain-the-competing-policies-20181115-h17ybu.

Keynes JM (1924) *A Tract on Monetary Reform*. London: Macmillan.

Keynes JM (1936) *The General Theory of Employment, Interest and Money*. London: Harcourt, Brace and Company.

Kohler C (2018) 'Majority of first-home buyers now use "Bank of Mum and Dad"', www.domain.com.au/money-markets/majority-of-firsthome-buyers-now-use-bank-of-mum-and-dad-20180502-h0zjun-432274/.

Konings M (2009) 'Rethinking neoliberalism and the subprime crisis: beyond the re-regulation agenda', *Competition and Change* 13(2): 108–27.

Konings M (2018) *Capital and Time: For a New*

Critique of Neoliberalism. Stanford, CA: Stanford University Press.

Köppe S (2018) 'Passing it on: inheritance, co-residence and the influence of parental support on homeownership and housing pathways', *Housing Studies* 33(2): 224–6.

Krause-Frantzen M (2019) *Going Nowhere, Slow: The Aesthetics and Politics of Depression*. Croydon: Zero Books.

Krippner GR (2011) *Capitalizing on Crisis: The Political Origins of the Rise of Finance*. Cambridge, MA: Harvard University Press.

Kuttner R (1980) *Revolt of the Haves: Tax Rebellions and Hard Times*. New York: Simon and Schuster.

La Cava G, Leal H & Zurawski A (2017) 'Housing accessibility for first home buyers', *Reserve Bank of Australia Bulletin* December: 19–28.

Laffer A, Moore S & Tanous P (2009) *The End of Prosperity: How Higher Taxes Will Doom the Economy – If We Let It Happen*. New York: Simon and Schuster.

Lambert P & Bihagen E (2014) 'Using occupation-based social classifications', *Work, Employment and Society* 28(3): 481–94.

Lamont M (1992) *Money, Morals and Manners: The Culture of the French and the American Upper-Middle Class*. Chicago, IL: University of Chicago Press.

Lapavitsas C (2009) 'Financialized capitalism: crisis and financial expropriation', *Historical Materialism* 17(2): 117–48.

Lapavitsas C (2014) *Profiting without Producing: How Finance Exploits Us All*. London and New York: Verso.

Lazonick W (2009) *Sustainable Prosperity in the New Economy? Business Organization and High-Tech*

Employment in the United States. Kalamazoo, MI: WE Upjohn Institute for Employment Research.

Lazzarato M (2011) *The Making of the Indebted Man.* Los Angeles, CA: Semiotext(e).

Lazzarato M (2015) *Governing by Debt.* Los Angeles, CA: Semiotext(e).

Leyshon A & Thrift N (2007) 'The capitalization of almost everything: the future of finance and capitalism', *Theory, Culture & Society* 24(7–8): 97–115.

Liu EY, Easthope H, Judd B & Burnley I (2015) 'Housing multigenerational households in Australian cities: evidence from Sydney and Brisbane at the turn of the twenty-first century'. In: Dufty-Jones R & Rogers D (eds.) *Housing in Twenty-First Century Australia: People, Practices and Policies.* Aldershot: Ashgate.

Lury C (2013) 'Topological sense-making: walking the mobius strip from cultural topology to topological culture', *Space and Culture* 16(2): 128–32.

Lury C, Parisi L & Terranova T (2012) 'Introduction: the becoming topological of culture', *Theory, Culture and Society* 29(4–5): 3–35.

Manish GP & O'Reilly C (2019) 'Banking regulation, regulatory capture and inequality', *Public Choice* 180(1): 145–64.

Mannheim K (1952 [1923]) 'The problem of generations'. In: Kecskemeti P (ed.) *Essays on the Sociology of Knowledge: Collected Works, Volume 5.* New York: Routledge.

Martin R (2002) *Financialization of Daily Life.* Philadelphia, PA: Temple University Press.

McCarty N (2013) 'Complexity, capacity, and capture'. In: Carpenter D & Moss DA (eds.) *Preventing Regulatory Capture: Special Interest Influence and How to Limit It.* Cambridge: Cambridge University Press.

McClanahan A (2019) 'Life expectancies: mortality, exhaustion, and economic stagnation', *Theory & Event* 22(2): 360–81.

McGovern P, Hill S, Mills C & White M (2007) *Market, Class and Employment.* Oxford: Oxford University Press.

Medhurst J (2014) *That Option No Longer Exists: Britain 1974–76.* Croydon: Zero Books.

Mehrling P (1999) 'The vision of Hyman P. Minsky', *Journal of Economic Behavior & Organization* 39(2): 129–58.

Michelmore M (2012) *Tax and Spend: The Welfare State, Tax Politics, and the Limits of American Liberalism.* Philadelphia, PA: University of Pennsylvania Press.

Milanovic B (2018) *Global Inequality: A New Approach for the Age of Globalization.* Cambridge, MA: Harvard University Press.

Minarik J (1980) *Who Doesn't Bear the Tax Burden?* Washington, DC: Brookings Institution.

Minsky H (1982) *Can 'It' Happen Again?* New York: M.E. Sharpe.

Minsky H (1996) 'Uncertainty and the institutional structure of capitalist economies: remarks upon receiving the Veblen-Commons Award', *Journal of Economic Issues* 30(2): 357–68.

Minsky H (2008 [1986]) *Stabilizing an Unstable Economy.* New York: McGraw Hill.

Mirowski P (2013) *Never Let a Serious Crisis Go to Waste: How Neoliberalism Survived the Financial Meltdown.* London and New York: Verso.

Muniesa F (2011) 'A flank movement in the understanding of valuation'. In: Adkins L & Lury C (eds.) *Measure and Value.* Oxford: Blackwell.

Muniesa F (2016) 'Setting the habit of capitalization: the pedagogy of earning power at the Harvard

Business School, 1920–1940', *Historical Social Research* 41(2): 196–217.

Muniesa F, Doganova L, Ortiz H, Pina-Stranger A, Paterson F, Bourgoin A, Ehrenstein V, Juven P-A, Pontille D, Sarac-Lesavre B & Yon G (2017) *Capitalization: A Cultural Guide*. Paris: Presses des Mines.

Naidu S (2017) 'A political economy take on W/Y'. In: Boushey H, Delong JB & Steinbaum M (eds.) *After Piketty: The Agenda for Economics and Inequality*. Cambridge, MA: Harvard University Press.

Negri A (1999) 'Value and affect', *boundary 2* 26(2): 77–88.

OECD (2018) *A Broken Social Elevator? How to Promote Social Mobility*. Paris: OECD Publishing.

Oliver D, McDonald P, Stewart A & Hewitt A (2016) *Unpaid Work Experience in Australia: Prevalence, Nature and Impact*. Canberra, ACT: Commonwealth Department of Employment.

Onaran O, Stockhammer E & Grafl L (2011) 'Financialisation, income distribution and aggregate demand in the USA', *Cambridge Journal of Economics* 35(4): 637–61.

Ong R, Jefferson T, Austen S, Haffner M & Wood G (2014) 'Housing equity withdrawal in Australia', *AHURI Research and Policy Bulletin* 176 (August). Melbourne, Vic: Australian Housing and Urban Research Institute Limited.

Ong R & Wood G (2019) 'More people are retiring with high mortgage debts. The implications are huge', *The Conversation*, 12 June, www.theconversation.com/more-people-are-retiring-with-high-mortgage-debts-the-implications-are-huge-115134.

Palley T (2012) *From Financial Crisis to Stagnation: The Destruction of Shared Prosperity and the Role of Economics*. Cambridge: Cambridge University Press.

Parkinson S, Rowley S, Stone W, James A, Spinney A & Reynolds M (2019) *Young Australians and the Housing Aspirations Gap*. Melbourne, Vic: Australian Housing and Urban Research Institute Limited.

Phillips K (1990) *The Politics of Rich and Poor: Wealth and the American Electorate in the Reagan Aftermath*. New York: HarperPerennial.

Phillips K (2003) *Wealth and Democracy*. New York: Broadway.

Piketty T (2014) *Capital in the Twenty-First Century*. Cambridge, MA: Harvard University Press.

Pixley J, Whimster S & Wilson S (2013) 'Central bank independence: a social economic and democratic critique', *The Economic and Labour Relations Review* 24(1): 32–50.

Quiggin J (2004) 'Economic policy'. In: Manne R (ed.) *The Howard Years*. Melbourne, Vic: Black Inc.

Reay D (1998) *Class Work: Mothers' Involvement in Their Children's Primary Schooling*. London: UCL Press.

Reeves RV (2018) *Dream Hoarders*. Washington, DC: Brookings Institution Press.

Reich R (1991) *The Work of Nations: Preparing Ourselves for 21st Century Capitalism*. New York: Random House.

Resolution Foundation (2018) *A New Generational Contract: The Final Report of the Intergenerational Commission*. London: Resolution Foundation.

Review of Business Taxation (1999) *A Tax System Redesigned, More Certain, Equitable and Durable (The Ralph Report), July*. Canberra, ACT: Australian Government Publishing Service.

Reynolds A (1999) *Capital Gains Tax: Analysis of Reform Options for Australia*. Washington, DC: Hudson Institute.

Roberts C, Blakeley G & Murphy L (2018) *A Wealth of Difference: Reforming the Taxation of Wealth*. London: Institution for Public Policy Research (IPPR).

Rognlie M (2015) 'Deciphering the fall and rise of the new capital share', *Brookings Papers on Economic Activity* Spring: 1–54.

Ronald R & Lennartz C (2018) 'Housing careers, inter-generational support and family relations', *Housing Studies* 33(2): 147–59.

Ronald R, Lennartz C & Kadi J (2017) 'What ever happened to asset-based welfare? Shifting approaches to housing wealth and welfare security', *Policy and Politics* 45(2): 173–93.

Rosa H (2013) *Social Acceleration: A New Theory of Modernity*. New York: Columbia University Press.

Rose D & Harrison E (eds.) (2011) *Social Class in Europe: An Introduction to the European Socioeconomic Classification*. Abingdon: Routledge.

Ryan-Collins J (2018) *Why Can't You Afford a Home?* Cambridge: Polity.

Ryan-Collins J, Lloyd T & Macfarlane L (2017) *Rethinking the Economics of Land and Housing*. London: Zed Books.

Savage M (2014) 'Piketty's challenge for sociology', *The British Journal of Sociology* 65(4): 591–606.

Savage M (2016) 'The fall and rise of class analysis in British sociology, 1950–2016', *Tempo Social, Revista de Sociologia da USP* 28(2): 57–72.

Savage M, Cunningham N, Devine F, Friedman S, Laurison D, McKenzie L, Miles A, Snee H & Wakeling P (2015) *Social Class in the 21st Century*. London: Penguin.

Savage M, Devine F, Cunningham N, Taylor M, Yaojun L, Hjelbrekke J, Le Roux B, Friedman S & Miles A

(2013) 'A new model of social class? Findings from the BBC's great British class survey experiment', *Sociology* 47(2): 219–50.

Schuldes M (2011) *Retrenchment in the American Welfare State: The Reagan and Clinton Administrations in Comparative Respective.* Münster: LIT Verlag.

Schwartz H & Seabrooke L (eds.) (2009) *The Politics of Housing Booms and Busts.* Basingstoke: Palgrave.

Seely A (2010) *Capital Gains Tax: The 2008 Reforms. Standard Note: SN4652, 3 June.* London: House of Commons Library.

Shackle GLS (1972) *Epistemics and Economics: A Critique of Economic Doctrines.* Cambridge: Cambridge University Press.

Shaw R (2018) *Generation Priced Out: Who Gets to Live in the New Urban America.* Oakland, CA: University of California Press.

Shepherd J (2016) *Crisis? What Crisis? The Callaghan Government and the British 'Winter of Discontent'.* Oxford: Oxford University Press.

Sheppard J & Biddle N (2017) 'Class, capital and identity in Australian society', *Australian Journal of Political Science* 52(4): 500–16.

Sherman R (2017) *Uneasy Street: The Anxieties of Affluence.* Princeton, NJ: Princeton University Press.

Sherraden M (2005) 'Assets and public policy'. In: Sherraden M (ed.) *Inclusion in the American Dream: Assets, Poverty, and Public Policy.* Oxford: Oxford University Press.

Silk L (1972) 'McGovern tax proposals examined', *New York Times*, 5 July.

Simon J & Stone T (2017) *The Property Ladder after the Financial Crisis.* Research Discussion Paper 5,

Economic Research Department, Reserve Bank of Australia.

Skeggs B (1997) *Formations of Class and Gender.* London: Sage.

Skerrett K, Weststar J, Archer S & Roberts C (eds.) (2017) *The Contradictions of Pension Fund Capitalism.* Ithaca, NY: Cornell University Press.

Soederberg S (2014) *Debtfare States and the Poverty Industry: Money, Discipline and the Surplus Population.* Abingdon: Routledge.

Southwood I (2011) *Non-Stop Inertia.* Winchester: Zero Books.

Standing G (2011) *The Precariat: The New Dangerous Class.* London: Bloomsbury.

Standing G (2016) *The Corruption of Capitalism: Why Rentiers Thrive and Work Does Not Pay.* London: BiteBack Publishing.

Stein S (2019) *Capital City: Gentrification and the Real Estate State.* London and New York: Verso.

Sternberg J (2019) *The Theft of a Decade: How the Baby Boomers Stole the Millennials' Economic Future.* New York: PublicAffairs.

Stilwell F (2019) *The Political Economy of Inequality.* Cambridge: Polity.

Strange S (1988) *States and Markets.* London: Pinter.

Streeck W (2014) *Buying Time: The Delayed Crisis of Democratic Capitalism.* London and New York: Verso.

Summers L (2016) 'The age of secular stagnation: what it is and what to do about it', *Foreign Affairs* March–April: 2–9.

Switzer T (2019) 'Anxiety plus ignorance: why millennials are embracing socialism', *Sydney Morning Herald*, 23 February.

Sydney Morning Herald (2004) 'Howard's crackpot capital gains tax reforms fail', 6 September.

Tadiar NXM (2012) 'Life-times in fate playing', *South Atlantic Quarterly* 111(4): 783–802.

Tadiar NXM (2013) 'Life-times of disposability within global neoliberalism', *Social Text* 35(1): 19–48.

The Economist (2019) 'Millennial socialism', 14 February.

Thrift N (2008) *Non-Representational Theory: Space, Politics, Affect.* Abingdon: Routledge.

Udagawa C & Sanderson P (2017) *The Impacts of Family Support on Access to Homeownership for Young People in the UK.* London: Social Mobility Commission.

US Census Bureau (2019) *Homeownership Rate for the United States* [RHORUSQ156N]. Federal Reserve Bank of St Louis, www.fred.stlouisfed.org/series/RHORUSQ156N.

Watlington C (2019) 'Who owns tomorrow?' *Commune 3*, www.communemag.com/who-owns-tomorrow/.

Weber R (2015) *From Boom to Bubble: How Finance Built the New Chicago.* Chicago, IL: University of Chicago Press.

Willetts D (2010) *The Pinch: How the Baby Boomers Took Their Children's Future – And Why They Should Give It Back.* London: Atlantic Books.

Willetts D (2019) 'Intergenerational warfare: who stole the millennials' future?', *Financial Times*, 2 July.

Wolff EN (1993) 'The rich get increasingly richer', Economic Policy Institute Briefing Paper.

Wolff EN (2014) 'Household wealth trends in the United States, 1983–2010', *Oxford Review of Economic Policy* 30(1): 21–43.

Wood D & Griffiths K (2019) *Generation Gap: Ensuring a Fair Go for Younger Australians.* Melbourne, Vic: Grattan Institute.

Woodman D & Wyn J (2015) *Youth and Generation:*

Rethinking Change and Inequality in the Lives of Young People. London: Sage.

Woodward B (1994) *The Agenda: Inside the Clinton White House.* New York: Simon and Schuster.

Wray RL (2016) *Why Minsky Matters: An Introduction to the Work of a Maverick Economist.* Princeton, NJ: Princeton University Press.

Wright EO (1978) *Class, Crisis and the State.* London: New Left Review.

Wright EO (1979) *Class Structure and Income Determination.* New York: Academic Press.

Wright EO (1985) *Classes.* London: Verso.

Wright EO (1997) *Class Counts: Comparative Studies in Class Analysis.* Cambridge: Cambridge University Press.

Wright EO (1998 [1989]) 'A general framework for the analysis of class structure'. In: Wright EO (ed.) *The Debate on Classes.* London: Verso.

Wright Mills C (1959) *The Sociological Imagination.* Oxford: Oxford University Press.

Yeates C (2016) 'NAB and Westpac say more parents guaranteeing kids' loans', *Sydney Morning Herald,* 23 November.

Zaloom C (2019) *Indebted: How Families Make College Work at Any Cost.* Princeton, NJ: Princeton University Press.

Index